Doing Theology

in a

Revolutionary Situation

DOING THEOLOGY

IN A

REVOLUTIONARY

SITUATION

JOSE MIGUEZ BONINO

FORTRESS PRESS

Philadelphia

Library of Congress Catalog Card Number 74-80424

ISBN 0-8006-1451-8

Ninth printing 1989

3965B89   Printed in the United States of America   1-1451

Contents

Editor's Foreword

Confrontation Books aim to confront the involved reader with the cross of Christ amid the crossroads of life. Confrontations are central to Christianity: both at the cross, for the content of Christian faith, and at the crossroads, for the context of Christian love. To enable responsible men to confront both life in Christ and Christ in life is the dialectical hallmark of authentic Christian theology.

Paul sharply contrasts two opposing types of theology: that of the contemplation of heaven and that of confrontation in the world. Theology can describe either man's search for God or God's search for man. Our choice determines our method.

If man's basic problem is considered to be his ignorance as a finite creature, then knowledge of God may properly be sought through man's rational speculation. If, rather, man's essential dilemma is confessed to be his idolatry as a proud and disobedient sinner, then knowledge of God can be achieved only through God's gracious self-revelation. Paul's gospel was regarded as scandalous by the religious men of his day precisely because he rejected man-centered contemplation in the name of Christ-centered confrontation: "When the time had fully come, God sent forth his Son. . . . Formerly, when you did not know God, you were in bondage to beings that by nature are not gods, but now . . . you have come to know God, or rather to be known by God" (Gal. 4:8-9).

Ours is therefore a *theology of worldly confrontation:* "God was in Christ reconciling the world to himself." No biblical theme is more promising for Christian renewal than the liberating gospel of God's ministry of reconciliation, grounded in Christ's cross and proclaimed by Christ's Church. In opposition to the rash of recent religious fads, the hidden lordship of the crucified Christ still constitutes the heart of the apostolic good news.

In a frightened and confused age, "Christ-figures" and "redemptive movements" rise and fall almost weekly. They pass by in dizzying succession in response to post-modern man's futile attempts to match his technological prowess in a shrinking world with some commensurate form of ideological universalism. However, the cross of the one unique Christ—Jesus of Nazareth—remains faith's unswerving answer to the institutional church's present "identity crisis": its seeming inability to become lovingly *identified with* the world without also becoming faithlessly *identical to* the world. Our suffering theology is no substitute for God's "suffering servant." We need to recapture that paradoxical unity of universality and particularity that undergirds Paul's gospel of God's reconciling work in Jesus of Nazareth, the Second Adam, who incorporates a new humanity into a new covenant with life's Lord.

Ours is also an *ethic of worldly confrontation:* "As you did it to one of the least of these my brethren, you did it to me." Apathetic Christians need to be reminded that Christ-centered reconciliation must always be viewed in the light of God's righteousness and judgment. Christian reconciliation in an evil world has nothing to do with either noncommittal neutrality or uninvolved appeasement.

Although Jesus surely died for all men, he also lived especially for some—the poor, the weak, the dispossessed, "the least of these my brethren." The Church, as the reconciling body of the risen Christ, is called to minister likewise. All men are sinners before a righteous God, but not all men are victims in an unjust society. This demands that we clearly distinguish, without falsely separating or equating, the Church and the world. Our

Christian hope lies in neither the secularization of the Church nor the sacralization of the world. Rather, the Church's worldly stance must remain in evangelical tension: strictly impartial in faith as it serves all sinful men alike in its ministry of Word and sacrament, yet compassionately partial in love as it struggles on behalf of God's suffering "have-nots" in its ministry of mercy and justice.

Confrontation Books, committed to man's personal confrontation with the cross of Christ amid the crossroads of life, will engage in down-to-earth theology in fidelity to a down-to-earth Lord. Readers are invited to think theologically (in depth before God) about the actual problems of life that confront them daily.

Our age, especially, challenges Christian theology to authenticate itself by responding humanely to the host of medical, political, racial, and military threats and opportunities facing mankind. In Confrontation Books, therefore, ecumenical authors of various churches, races, nationalities, and professions will seek to develop current Christian lifestyles by confronting with biblical insights and theological affirmations of faith controversial secular problems—e.g., pollution, heroin, revolution, and nuclear warfare illumined by man as God's image, Christ as man's liberator, the Church as sign of the world's unity, and the Kingdom as God's reign among men.

We seek thereby to demonstrate the truth of Luther's words, "Not reading and speculation, but living, dying, and being condemned make a real theologian."

In this volume the theology of liberation is surveyed and evaluated by one of its foremost participant-critics in Latin America, Jose Miguez Bonino of Argentina. Interest in this movement has grown rapidly in North America, both because of its own importance and because of related developments among the proponents of black and women's liberation theology.

The influential journal *Christianity and Crisis* sponsored a fascinating discussion for North Americans on the theology of liberation. No less than three issues were devoted to various aspects of the theme, with theologians, ethicists, political scientists and economists joining in the running debate.[1] Theological highlights of that debate will help to sharpen the reader's critical appraisal of Professor Miguez Bonino's own survey.

The theology of liberation is the most recent and important attempt by Latin American Christians to relate current theological perspectives to ethical responsibility for the many problems of their region. Though only about six years old, its outlook influenced the important message of the Latin American Bishops Conference at Medellín, Colombia in 1968, and it completely oriented the manifesto issued by Christians for socialism in Santiago, Chile in 1972.[2]

With this impressive claim, the debate was initiated by Thomas G. Sanders, a Christian ethicist specializing in church-state relations, who has worked much of the last decade with American University Field Service in Latin America.[3] Far more controversial is Sanders's charge that both the presuppositions and the social analysis of liberation theology are forms of the moralistic, "soft" utopianism already rejected in the school of "Christian Realism" of *Christianity and Crisis*'s eminent founder, Reinhold Niebuhr, and his theological disciples.

Sanders interprets liberation theology as "an ethical theology that grew out of social awareness and the desire to act."[4] Quoting from Gutiérrez's *A Theology of Liberation,* he describes it as "a theological reflection born of the experience of shared

1. *Christianity and Crisis; A Christian Journal of Opinion* (New York: September 17, 1973; October 15, 1973; November 26, 1973), *passim.*
2. "The Theology of Liberation: Christian Utopianism," *Christianity and Crisis,* September 17, 1973, p. 167.
3. Political ethics is also the subject of Dr. Sanders's earlier work, *Protestant Concepts of Church and State; Historical Backgrounds and Approaches for the Future* (New York: Doubleday Anchor Books, 1965).
4. Sanders, "The Theology of Liberation," p. 168.

efforts to abolish the current unjust situation and to build a different society, freer and more human."[5]

Liberation theology, reflecting the influence of Roman Catholic thinkers Pierre Teilhard de Chardin and Johannes Metz along with Protestants Jürgen Moltmann and Wolfhart Pannenberg, replaces the traditional natural law ethic of Catholicism with the organizing theme and dynamic of "liberation." Gutiérrez emphasizes three means of liberation, all of which are interdependent, comprising a single, complex process that finds its deepest sense and its full realization in the saving work of Jesus Christ:

(1) The aspiration of oppressed people and social groups to escape the domination of wealthy countries and oppressive classes.

(2) An understanding of history in which man assumes conscious responsibility for his own destiny, leading to "the creation of a new man and a qualitatively different society."

(3) The transformation of man through encounter with Jesus Christ. "Christ the Savior liberates man from sin, which is the ultimate root of all disruption of friendship and of all injustice and oppression."[6]

The biblical theme of the Kingdom of God provides the universal framework within which the liberation of Christians and other human beings takes place. For Gutiérrez and his associates, the close link between salvation and justice serves to unify all events of liberation within the expanding Kingdom of God. He writes in a significant passage:

The growth of the Kingdom is a process that occurs historically in liberation, insofar as liberation means a greater fulfillment of man. . . . While liberation is implemented in liberating historical events, it also denounces their limitations and ambiguities, pro-

5. Gustavo Gutiérrez, *A Theology of Liberation; History, Politics and Salvation* (Maryknoll, New York: Orbis Books, 1973). Translated and edited by Sister Caridad Inda and John Eagleson from *Teología de la liberación, Perspectivas* (Lima: CEP, 1971).
6. Ibid.

claims their fulfillment and impels them effectively toward total communion. This is not an identification. Without liberating historical events, there would be no growth of the Kingdom. But the process of liberation will not have conquered the very roots of oppression and the exploitation of man by man without the Kingdom of God, which is above all a gift.[7]

Having traced these basic perspectives, Sanders turns next to the ethical responsibility of Latin American Christians that is advocated by liberation theology. Marxism, socialism, and utopianism represent Gutiérrez's chief weapons of implementation.[8]

Marxism is employed "to reflect on the meaning of the transformation of the world and the action of man in history." Class struggle is a daily reality toward which Christians cannot be neutral: one is with either the oppressed or the oppressors. The Marxist view of history spotlights the public arena of conflict: "the division of humanity into oppressors and oppressed, into owners of the means of production and those dispossessed of the fruits of their work, into antagonistic social classes."

Socialism is championed as the vehicle for Latin American liberation. Liberation theology rejects any solutions from outside in the form of "Christian principles" or guidelines from natural law. Instead it chooses to identify with and participate in an already emergent political process. Sanders cites the alternatives posed by the manifesto of the Christians for socialism ("a dependent and underdeveloped capitalism or socialism"), as well as the conviction of Gutiérrez: "Only a radical break from the status quo, access to power of the exploited class and a social revolution that would break this dependence would allow for the change to a new society, a socialist society—or at least allow such a society to be possible."

Utopianism is embraced and interpreted positively to provide a vision for radical change. Utopia, writes Gutiérrez,

7. Ibid.
8. Sanders, "The Theology of Liberation," p. 169, *passim.*

"leads to an authentic and scientific knowledge of reality and to a praxis that transforms what exists." Moreover, it also "postulates, enriches and supplies new goals for political action, while at the same time it is verified by this action."

On the basis of this total orientation, Thomas Sanders charges that liberation theology lends itself to

> a moralistic ideology in utopian form as a reaction to a legalistic and conservative ethic, guilt over the complicity of the church in social evils, discovery of the radicalness of biblical ethics and dialogue with non-Christian movements of social criticism like Marxism. Latin American Christianity has passed through these creative but painful experiences during the past decade, just as North American Protestantism underwent them earlier in this century.[9]

Sanders identifies with the objection to utopian moralism that he sees rooted in "the Pauline-Augustinian-Lutheran tradition," as reformulated in Reinhold Niebuhr's repudiation of the Social Gospel movement in the liberal wing of North American Protestantism.

Two principle weaknesses are cited.[10] First, utopian moralism contradicts "the biblical view of human nature and history." On the one hand, sin persists in the life of the redeemed. Though liberated by Christ from sin, Christians continue to engage in selfishness and injustice. There is no Christian politics, only Christians in politics. On the other hand, history is likewise not an upward advance in moral progress. There is a tragic dimension to human existence that continually corrupts political events in dialectic and paradox.

Second, utopian moralism "gives insufficient consideration to the moral ambiguity that characterizes all forms of social existence." Every government or social system is imperfect and will continue to be so. "Achievements of justice and freedom do not flow smoothly from the good will of individuals but from a precarious balance of power in a given social context."

9. Ibid., p. 170.
10. Ibid.

As a former sympathizer of Marxism, Niebuhr grew to reject too close an alliance between Christianity and any secular movement of partisan protest. Marxism, in particular, is both less scientific and more self-righteous than it purports to be, whenever it attempts to put its "moralistic dichotomies" into political and economic practice.

Sanders therefore concludes his critique of liberation theology as a Christian Realist with the claim:

> No Latin American decision-maker can base his judgments on liberation or the Kingdom of God. Rather, he must make complex, morally ambiguous judgments on the basis of national interest, the pressure of the groups supporting him, or commitments to national goals such as increasing economic production or solving urban problems.[11]

Three theological ethicists were invited by the editors of *Christianity and Crisis* to respond to Sanders's analysis: Rubem A. Alves, John C. Bennett, and Robert McAfee Brown. Their views will be summarized more briefly, since they all identified more positively with the orientation developed at length in the present study of Professor Miguez Bonino.

Rubem Alves counterattacks in four points while characterizing the "fatalistic undertone" of Christian Realism as representing the "ideology of the Establishment."[12]

First, he maintains that concepts like "liberation" and the "Kingdom of God" do not evidence "a belief in the possibility of a perfect society but rather the belief in the nonnecessity of *this* imperfect order." These themes are normative and not intended for direct policy application. Second, Alves contends that "reality is a human construction which can be demolished by men in order to create a new one." It is idolatrous to give

11. Ibid., p. 171.
12. "Christian Realism: Ideology of the Establishment," *Christianity and Crisis,* September 17, 1973, pp. 173 ff., *passim.* Dr. Alves is Professor of Philosophical Foundations of Social Sciences, Faculty of Philosophy, Science and Letters at the University of Rio Claro, Sao Paulo, Brazil. He is also the author of *A Theology of Human Hope* (Washington, D.C.: Corpus Books, 1969).

ultimacy—demonic or divine—to that which is merely human and provisional. Third, Christian utopianism is based on the vision that "all social systems are under God's historical judgment." It is therefore wrong to make these same systems the ultimate criteria for what is possible and impossible in history.

Finally, the Latin American concludes "in irritation" that Christian Realism is indebted to its own "silent agreements" with positivism and pragmatism. Alves challenges, "And when we say this, we are saying that the traditional ways of doing theology must recognize their ideological bias, their rather unambiguous relationships with colonialism, racism, and economic exploitation. We believe that your theology to a great degree—although it does not want to recognize this—is part of cultural imperialism."

John C. Bennett, a close colleague of Niebuhr's for many years, recalls that "Christian Realism in its early days had a much more dialectical view of the relation between the Kingdom of God and historical decisions or institutions than that which informs his [Sanders's] article."[13]

Bennett freely acknowledges that there are "some simplifications" and "strategic concentrations" in the theology of liberation. He also agrees that there is a lot of romantic talk about "the revolution," and that there is need to prepare for all the moral ambiguities inevitable in future developments in the abuses of power. Nevertheless, Bennett contends that support should be given at this moment in history to that "almost miraculous" change within a considerable part of the Roman Catholic Church in Latin America. Centering in the emphasis on "conscientization" in liberation theology, it demonstrates "the need for a revolutionary awareness of human dignity and

13. *Christianity and Crisis,* October 15, 1973, pp. 197-198. Dr. Bennett has taught Christian Ethics at Union Theological Seminary, New York, and at the Pacific School of Religion. He explored political issues in such earlier studies as *Christians and the State* (New York: Charles Scribner's Sons, 1958) and *Foreign Policy in Christian Perspective* (New York: Charles Scribner's Sons, 1966).

potentialities obscured by dehumanizing social conditions, an awareness of the reality of oppression and of the need for radical structural change."

Robert McAfee Brown concurs in his response, believing that "the proponents of liberation theology know a lot more about the temptation to abuse their own potential power than Sanders indicates."[14]

Brown notes, for example, that Gutiérrez (whose study he lauds as "the most important book of the year, or of the decade") argues his case with considerable theological sophistication. Gutiérrez works to prevent political liberation, in his own words,

> from being translated into any kind of Christian ideology of political action or [into] a politico-religious messianism. Christian hope opens us, in an attitude of spiritual childhood, to the gift of the future promised by God. It keeps us from any confusion of the Kingdom with any one historical stage, from any idolatry toward unavoidably ambiguous achievement, from any absolutizing of revolution.

Brown insists that North American Christians should be grateful to Latin American theologians for exposing their own political conditioning and societal prejudices. North American theology is not produced in a cultural vacuum and it shows. "White Americans," he charges, "always find it easy to attack likely abuses of power by someone else 'after the revolution' to the exclusion of attacking the abuses of power of which they and their nation are guilty 'before the revolution.'"

Thomas Sanders, in reply to his critics, recognizes especially the validity of John Bennett's response. He suggests a bi-focal truce in that "the social sciences are one way of looking at reality and Christianity is a different way. . . . Whatever, then, its immediate power possibilities, the real significance of the

14. Ibid., pp. 199, 200. Dr. Brown is Professor of Religion at Stanford University and investigates theological themes of the third world in two new studies published in 1974, *Religion and Violence* and *Frontiers for the Church Today*.

theology of liberation lies in its presence as a witness to what it represents."[15]

Sanders acknowledges that his own personal agenda in Latin America has increasingly "depended heavily on the social sciences," and that the "chief framework" of his writing has become "national power processes and programs . . . and the redistribution of power." He admits that his attempt to "social scientize" the theology of liberation loses, in effect, "the tension between the two ways of looking at reality." In his dismay at the exposure of his own faulty analytical tools (more realistic than Christian), Sanders never recovers enough to return to the original theological issue—the validity of the attempt of the theology of liberation to "eschatologize" the socialist revolution in Latin America.

In other words, Sanders comes to a belated awareness of the reality of another power at work among oppressed Latin American Christians: "the gospel: it is the power of God for salvation" (Rom. 1:16). Having acknowledged that reality, however, Sanders does not then vigorously pursue the theological question of whether this "dynamite (*dunamis*) of God" in salvatory power is different in kind, or form, or fulfillment, or at all, from the political and economic power realities in Latin American society today. Does liberation theology truly come to grips with both the radicality of man's sin and the miraculous quality of God's grace that prompted great Christian thinkers in the past to grapple with the dialectical relation of the City of Man and the City of God (Augustine), natural and divine law (Aquinas), civil and Christian righteousness (Luther), common and saving grace (Calvin)?

What did Jesus mean when he apparently proclaimed both that "The Kingdom of God is in your midst" (or, "within you"), and also that "My kingship is not from this world" (Luke 17:21; John 19:36)? To employ the categories of our

15. *Christianity and Crisis,* November 26, 1973, pp. 249 ff.

inquiry, does Christianity offer us a theology of liberation and/ or an ethic of liberation? If the former, then why didn't Jesus simply identify with the power politics of the Zealots of his day? If the latter, then how do we now properly relate Christian eschatology (or biblical eschatologies!) to the power politics of our day?

The decisive issue for liberation theology is the relation of Christian freedom to political liberty. By what apostolic authority may we conflate liberation from sin, death, and the demonic, with liberation from injustice, oppression, and poverty? In more personal terms, how do we relate the first-century activities of Jesus and Paul with the twentieth-century activities of Ché Guevara and Camilo Torres? Are they similar, repetitious, distinguishable, or unrelated?

These are some of the unanswered questions explored in Professor Miguez Bonino's penetrating analysis. Our sole concern is to broaden the ecumenical basis for common Christian praxis as widely as possible. Liberation in Latin America is a divine imperative; conscientious participation is our common calling. That last word belongs properly to Gustavo Gutiérrez:

> To paraphrase a well-known text of Pascal, we can say that all the political theologies, the theologies of hope, of revolution, and of liberation, are not worth one act of genuine solidarity with exploited social classes. They are not worth one act of faith, love, and hope, committed—in one way or another—in active participation to liberate man from everything that dehumanizes him and prevents him from living according to the will of the Father.[16]

Philadelphia, Pennsylvania　　　　WILLIAM H. LAZARETH
Advent, 1974

16. Gutiérrez, *A Theology of Liberation*, p. 308.

Preface

In the time that has elapsed between beginning to write this book and its publication, the theology of liberation tends to be a new "consumer good" in the European-North American theological market. It is, therefore, with a certain reluctance and uneasiness that I add one more book to the thousands of pages of articles, books, and dissertations already published. On the other side, the ghastly events which are taking place in Chile have provided a painful reminder—if it was necessary—that the struggle for the liberation of the Latin American (and the third world) societies is as urgent as ever, but a long road strewed with suffering, sacrifice, and death.

To the extent that the theology of liberation is—and is made into—a new "school," a set of self-contained theological tenets or positions, it will have its day and be gone. As a matter of fact, the pioneers in this movement are more and more unhappy with the very expression *theology of liberation*. But to the extent that we are here dealing with a task, the struggle for liberation, which lies as much ahead of us as ten or five years ago, which indeed in a certain sense always lies ahead of us, this task continues to be pertinent: a critical and committed Christian reflection of the people who have made this struggle their own and who understand it as the concrete witness to the freedom that has been promised to man in Jesus Christ. The reflection will take many forms—it will be discourse, hymn, prayer, or lament—and locations—in exile, in the classroom, in chapel, among urban or peasant guerrillas, in trade union or political party. But it will always strive for that unity which is forever a task, a prayer, and a hope: the full measure of manhood as it was in Jesus Christ.

It is this search under the conditions of dependent and dominated Latin America that we have tried to present. In this sense, the theology of liberation coming out of Latin America is a question addressed to the Christian obedience of our brethren in Christ elsewhere—a question, though, that only they can answer for themselves.

Buenos Aires, Argentina JOSE MIGUEZ BONINO
Spring, 1974

Introduction

In April, 1972, while the III UNCTAD (United Nations Commission for Trade and Development) was, rather unprofitably, debating the distorted terms of trade between the developed and the underdeveloped world, in the same city of Santiago, Chile, just across the street, four hundred Latin American Christians met for a quite different analysis of much the same problems. There were Catholics and Protestants, priests, nuns, a couple of bishops, ministers, and laymen, peasant leaders, university students and professors. Most of the significant Latin American theologians—men whose names and writings appear increasingly in international theological journals and books— were active participants. (A few, from Uruguay and Brazil notably, were absent not of their own will). The gathering called itself "Christians for socialism" and defined its own character in these terms:

> ... Christians who, starting from the process of liberation which our Latin American countries are undergoing and from our concrete and active engagement in the building of a socialist society, think out our faith and reexamine our attitude of love for the oppressed.[1]

Since its conception, this conference had unleashed a severe reaction. Several Catholic episcopates—including the Chilean one—disassociated themselves from it. Catholic and Protestant rightist movements denounced it in acid language. Some Latin American intelligence services carefully listed the participants and controlled their departure from and return to their respective countries. On the other hand, the international religious press followed the meeting with keen interest. North American and European observers were evident everywhere at the meeting. One of them hailed it as the most significant single event in the history of Latin American Christianity.[2] Another one called it "a qualitative break" in the self-understanding of Western Christianity.[3] One North American Board of Missions silently underwrote a large portion of the expenses.

A consideration of the nature, mood, and conclusions of this meeting is an excellent point of departure for a discussion of what is happening today in Christianity in general and in theological reflection in particular in the subcontinent south of the Rio Grande. It is my conviction that such a discussion—beyond what has been called "the boom of Latin American theology"—is of significance for a Christian's understanding of himself anywhere in the world. In more than twenty years of participation in denominational and ecumenical circles, I have been to many conferences, congresses, and theological colloquia. This one belongs, both in mood and nature, to a different order.

It was, quite obviously, a gathering of *militant* people. Most of them had paid their own way to Santiago, traveling in the least expensive way. They came from the shanty towns, the countryside, the industrial belts or the student unions of the large Latin American cities; they came from immediate participation in the struggles and conflicts of peasants, workers, and students. Not a few had recent experiences of persecution, jail, and torture. They were clearly committed to a purpose—the transformation of Latin American society, through revolutionary change, in the direction of a socialist society. They had come to find out how they could encourage, support, and help each other in the road toward this goal. They had come to explore and deepen together their understanding and commitment to this task. The air was dense with the dynamism and bouyancy of common purpose. Introductions were not necessary. The fellowship was there, objectively real, as air to be breathed, as you entered the meeting. To the same extent, protocol and diplomacy were absent. There was no need to explore tactfully the coincidences, to preface one's intervention with all sorts of disclaimers and qualifications. Time was too short and the business in hand too important and urgent. There was a briskness and a bluntness in the discussions which one seldom finds in other meetings. We did not expect to depart carrying a mere set of well-meaning resolutions but an adequate instrument for the struggle.

The concreteness of the questions posed and the answers sought, even in the most theoretical subjects, created a quite new relation between the intellectual "stars" and the rest of the meeting. Affirmations, however brilliant or clever, were supposed to be tested against everyday experience. The meeting had no patience with the classic game of posing an abstract question in order to fit a theoretical answer which one has already developed. It had first to be convinced that the question itself represented a real problem, the solution of which was demanded by a concrete and active engagement.

As, one after the other, the participants brought during the first two days an account of the struggle for liberation in their own countries, a moving picture of need, oppression, suffering, and repression was displayed before our eyes. But not of hopelessness or powerlessness.[4] There was sadness in front of so much unnecessary suffering. There was anger in the face of so much stupid hardness and deliberate wickedness. But underneath there was the deep joy and alert confidence of people who knew that they were not "beating the air" but fighting "a good battle." As I heard one of the national groups "witnessing," the verse of Acts came to my mind: "rejoicing that they were counted worthy of suffering. . . ."

Suffering . . . for whose sake? Fellowship . . . in what name? Commitment . . . to whom? For some of the critics the answer is easy and final: these men have surrendered to a (Marxist) ideology; they have mistaken revolution for the gospel; they have renounced the fellowship of the faith for the comradeship of political groups and parties. We shall have to deal later on with some of the questions involved in these accusations. For the moment, however, it is more important to realize that such criticisms miss altogether the self-understanding of the people involved. One of them wrote recently in this respect that Christians, engaged in this struggle,

> see such conflicts and criticisms as totally foreign and surprising. . . . They experience an evangelical renewal. They rediscover and re-value all the more traditional aspects of Christianity. . . . Not only do they not cease to be Christians but rather they experience a profound renewal of their faith and their Christian commitment. . . .[5]

What is this "new breed of Christians" as somebody has called them? Where do they come from? How have they arrived at the stance they now have? What account do they give of the gospel and of their own faith? How do they explain their action in terms of Christianity? Only time will say whether this "new way of being Christian" represents a genuine insight into the work of the Holy Spirit at this time in history, a new age in the march of the gospel across time or a miscarriage of prophecy, one of the no-exit detours into which Christians have more than once trapped themselves. Christians and non-Christians alike in Latin America are forced to respond to this new reality. By its very nature no one can remain neutral before it. It refuses to be merely assimilated in traditional categories or placed side by side with other religious "products" available in the market. If it is true, it demands a total overhaul of Christian piety, ecclesiastical institutions, discipline, and theological reflection. If it is wrong, it must be unmasked and exposed because it threatens to mislead and subvert at least a significant sector of Christianity.

The exploration of this new way is what we propose as the subject of the present study. It is done in the conviction that it is a meaningful and fruitful challenge to Christians everywhere, an authentic call to significant dialogue on the truth and the power of the gospel that, for the first time, Christians in Latin America address to their brethren of the rest of the world.

We shall attempt this exploration in two parts. In the first one we shall try to give an account of the new way from inside it, following its own dynamics and in its own terms. In the second part we will face critically some of the questions which this new way poses for theological thought. The author wants to be understood as one who moves, however critically, definitely along this road. To do it critically, constantly raising questions, is not in this case a restriction or qualification but rather a more definite commitment because a critical conscience is the very heart of the stance assumed. We are therefore not inviting the reader to a mere intellectual exercise or an interesting trip into an exotic corner of the Christian landscape. We are challenging him to respond to the call of Christ, who, we believe, is today summoning his people to a new departure in the understanding and obedience of the faith.

An understanding of what this new Christian consciousness means demands at least four areas of analysis. These will constitute the contents of the first part of the book. The first chapter tries to locate the movement historically, against the background of the fundamental stages in the history of Christianity in Latin America. It is one of our contentions, in fact, that there is no such thing as a Christianity outside or above its concrete temporal incarnations. These have taken place in our continent in two fundamental historical projects: Spanish colonialism (Roman Catholicism) and North Atlantic neocolonialism (Protestantism). A Christian can only understand himself in Latin America when he discovers, analyzes, and takes a stand concerning these historical relationships of his faith. The first "break" in the new Christian consciousness is the affirmation that we are moving beyond a colonial and a neocolonial Christianity, with all that this implies.

Such an affirmation, nevertheless, already presumes a certain analysis of our history and present situation; an analysis, namely, in sociopolitical categories. Even more, we are dealing with categories belonging to a sociological science indebted to Marxist analysis. This was explicitly affirmed at Santiago:

> The construction of socialism cannot be achieved by means of vague denunciations or appeals to good will, but rather presupposes an analysis that will highlight the mechanisms that really drive society. . . . Political action calls for a scientific analysis of reality because there is a continuous interrelation between action and analysis. . . .[6]

In the second chapter we attempt to develop the understanding of our situation by means of this analytical method because this diagnosis of reality underlies the concrete option in which faith and obedience are articulated.

We will follow this presentation with a discussion (third chapter) of the understanding of faith and obedience characterizing the new way. "This revolutionary commitment has made us discover the meaning of the liberating work of Christ," says the document.[7] This discovery has two sides. One is critical: it rereads the history of Christian piety, action, and thought through the means of analysis adopted in order to unmask and expose the ideological misuse of Christianity as a tool of oppression: "The alliance between Christianity and the dominant classes explains to a large extent the historical forms assumed by the Christian conscience." We must follow this criticism as it moves relentlessly through several areas of our traditional Western Christianity. But this is not an end in itself. It is the shadow of a positive commitment:

> Increasingly large numbers of Christians are now discovering the historical vigor of their faith as a result of their political action in the construction of socialism and the liberation of the continent's oppressed people. The Christian faith thus displays a new liberating and critical vitality.[8]

But this is understood not merely at a detachable, secular level.

Rather, this commitment is the matrix for a rediscovery of the true meaning of discipleship.

> The Christian committed to revolutionary practice discovers the liberating force of the love of God, of the death and resurrection of Christ. He discovers that his faith does not imply the acceptance of a world that is already made, or of a predetermined history, but rather that the very living of his faith involves the creation of a new and solidary world and leads to historical initiatives fertilized by Christian hopes.[9]

Commitment, therefore, is born of a rationality of social analysis and demands in turn to account for itself in theological terms. In this way "a new type of theological reflection" appears, integral with concrete social and political action. To this new type of reflection we shall devote the last chapter of our first part.

Is it possible to establish a meaningful dialogue between the new way and traditional theological concerns? It will certainly be a polemical and critical dialogue in many aspects. Its difficulty will be related not only to the instruments of analysis and the categories of expression used by the new and the traditional, but also—and mainly—to the forms of consciousness and the militancies to which (more or less consciously) each one is related. Nevertheless, it must be attempted for the sake of the health both of the new way and the old Christendom; a health which will have to be dearly bought, but which we must at all costs seek.

The second part of our book will attempt to gather around four theological nuclei some of the questions thrown by the analysis of the new way: the hermeneutical problem (the question of the interpretation of the gospel in our time), the relation of struggle and reconciliation, the eschatological dimension (the relation between the "new" which we want to build through direct political action and the "new" which the gospel promises) and the ecclesiological question (where is the Church to be found?). A chapter will be devoted to each of these problems. If to some extent we succeed to help the partners-adversaries genuinely to engage each other in this polemical dialogue, our purpose will have been fulfilled. Hopefully the Partner-Adversary who meets us in judgment and grace will lead us beyond the conflict, not merely in words and imagination, but in truth and reality.

NOTES

[1] "Documento Final," Introducción. The "Final Document" and the documentation of the meeting have been published in the official report *Cristianos por el Socialismo* (Santiago de Chile: Editorial "Mundo Nuevo," 1972). We quote from the "Documento Final" according to paragraphs. There is also a full documentation and the reports in the journal *Cristianismo y Sociedad* (Montevideo: Editorial "Tierra Nueva," Casilla de Correo 179), nos. 31/32 (1972). An English version has been published by IDOC (IDOC International, 30 Via S. Maria dell' Anima, Rome, Italy, 00186), *IDOC-Document* no. 48 (November, 1972). There are a good summary and background documentation in the Bulletin *Exchange* of the Department of Missiology of the "Interuniversity Institute for Missiological Research" (Boerhaavelaan 43, Leiden, The Netherlands), no. 6 (1973). An English version has also been produced in mimeographed form by James Goff (Apartado 5594, Lima 1, Perú).

[2] A critical discussion of the reactions and comments concerning the meeting will be found in *Cristianismo y Sociedad,* nos. 33/34 (1972). A number of reactions are also summarized in *Exchange* (see n. 1), pp. 40-51.

[3] Giulio Girardi, "Los cristianos y el socialismo; de Medellín a Santiago", in *Cristianos por el socialismo: Exigencias de una opción* (Montevideo: Editorial Tierra Nueva, 1973), p. 68. This book gathers the material published in *Cristianismo y Sociedad* (see ni. 2 above) and adds a complete bibliography of publications of the Santiago meeting and comments in Spanish, Italian, French, German, and English (pp. 161-165).

[4] The reports of the different delegations are published in *Cristianos por el socialismo,* pp. 67-174.

[5] J. Pablo Richard Guzman, "El significado histórico de la fe cristiana en la praxis revolucionaria," *Pasos* (Santiago de Chile: Bulletin of "Church and Society in Latin America," ISAL), no. 34 (January 22, 1973), p. 4.

[6] "Documento Final," Introducción, and part I, 1.1. Cf. also part II, 2.4.

[7] "Documento Final," Introducción.

[8] Ibid., part I, 3.4.   [9] Ibid., part II, 3.5.

Part One

A NEW BREED

OF CHRISTIANS?

Chapter One

Beyond Colonial and Neocolonial Christianity

Not long ago a group of young people from a shanty town in Uruguay was performing an improvised play in one of the well-to-do Protestant churches. In the conversation that followed between the actors and the congregation somebody asked the question: "Who, then, is Jesus Christ?" "For us," shot back immediately and spontaneously one of the group, "Jesus Christ is Ché Guevara." Once we get over the shock of the first impression of such an answer, it begins to dawn on us that, in the course of history, the face of Jesus Christ has frequently taken on the features of the man—ideal or historical—who best represented what at that moment men linked most closely with the Christian religion or with the fullness of humanity. In Latin America, just as in other places, these identifications had been quite common. This or that missionary or priest, or the suffering Indian or mixed blood, was cast as a model for the Christ. What is new and startling is that a group of Christians would name for that role a guerrilla fighter and, moreover, a man who was—quite consciously and lucidly—not a Christian but a Marxist revolutionary.

The attraction, nevertheless, is mutual. Guevara himself had said: "Only when Christians will have the courage to give a wholehearted revolutionary testimony will the Latin American revolution become invincible," and he added, "because up to the present they have allowed their doctrine to be instrumentalized by the reactionaries."[1] This is a curious sentence, because it seems to imply that revolution is a birthright for the Christians while reaction would be a travesty (an *instrumentalizing*) of their doctrine. This seems far from an orthodox Marxist interpretation of Christianity. If we interpret the words of the young Uruguayan in the context of Guevara's quote, they seem to me to mean at least three things, which represent a growing consensus among young Latin American Christians. They are saying:

(1) "A Jesus Christ who can be preached and worshiped outside the frame of reference indicated by the name of Guevara has no meaning or relevance for us—indeed, he becomes our enemy." In other words: a time in the history of the Christian faith, the pre-Guevara time, is closed and gone.

(2) "Guevara represents for us the world in which we live, the language we understand, the reality which is in us and around us—we live in the world of sociopolitical reality. If you will name the name of Jesus Christ, it must be within this world." In other words: a new territory is open for Christian mission.

(3) "What we discover in Guevara is linked with the name of Jesus Christ." Curiously enough, they did not say: "Ché Guevara is Christ," but "Christ is Ché Guevara." In other words: liberation and revolution are a legitimate transcription of the gospel.

How can we trace the succession of these periods or ages indicated in these comments in the history of Christianity (in our continent at least)? In a recent analysis of the Roman Catholic Church in Argentina, Lucio Gera speaks of three types in the leadership of his Church, who represent both different conceptions of the role of Christianity and different epochs in the history of the Latin American Church:[2]

(1) The "traditionalists," "rightists," or "conservatives," preaching "integralism" at their extreme. Their understanding

3

of the Church and the faith goes back to the time of the Spanish colonization and is nourished by the ideal of "Christendom." This is expressed in the desire for a close unity between Church and state ("a religio-political monism") and the ideal of colonial Christianity, rejecting all modifications of the institutions. In modern times this current expressed itself as "an aristocratic Catholic nationalism" which was strong until the fifties and survives today in small but belligerent reactionary groups.

(2) A "progressive" tendency, which traces its origin to "enlightened" currents in Spain, and later to the French Enlightenment. It incorporated later on the "Christian democratic" movements and recently the progressive European theology which was influential in Vatican II. It looks to Europe for its inspiration. While it tends to adopt reformist or developmentalist positions in sociopolitical questions, its thrust is for the internal renewal of the Church and a clear distinction between the religious and the political areas (and consequently between Church and state).

(3) A "revolutionary" Catholicism which originated in the sixties, but can also claim the heritage of "social protest" of some priests in the colonial and emancipation times. It disengages itself from reformist views and moves beyond the separation of religious and political areas, while rejecting any form of theocratic synthesis.

Christianity entered Latin America under two historic movements: conquest and colonization in the sixteenth century and modernization and neocolonialism in the nineteenth.

"In carrying out the enterprise of the Indies [i.e., discovering the new world]," wrote Columbus, "it was not reason, or mathematics, or charts that helped me; the discovery was simply a fulfillment of what Isaiah had said."[3] He refers to the promise that God would lead the ships of Tarshish to bring the treasures and glory of the nations to the sanctuary of the Lord. To annex a territory to the crown of Spain and to bring it to the altar of the Lord were one and the same thing; the cause of

Jesus Christ and the cause of Spain were identical for that country which had just completed "under the banner of the Catholic faith" the expulsion of the Moslems from its territory and the unification of the kingdom. The new world just discovered gave them the opportunity to bring to earth the old utopia, the dream of "the Christian Kingdom," an ideal order which would embody the sacred temporal order and the ecclesiastical divine order, both of them structured to their minor details in Scholastic thought. Conquest and evangelization are, in the mind of both the political leaders and the Catholic hierarchy of Spain, one single project. "We come from Castile," might run one of the standard speeches of the conquest to the Indians, "where reigns a most powerful king. . . . We set out to subject the lands which we find to our king. It is our chief desire to make you realize that you worship false gods and that you need to worship the only God who is in heaven."[4] Obedience to the great king of Spain and submission to the King of heaven were demanded as one single act.

The dream was, of course, never realized. All the realities of history and geography—long distances, the scarcity of priests, the persistence of the old indigenous culture and religion, the hunger for gold and wealth, human frailty, the self-perpetuating inertia of sociopolitical structures conspired against it. What in reality took place was the extension to America and the adaptation here of the form of semifeudal (seigneurial) society that existed in Spain. This order prescribed the two basic elements of the social structure in the new world: land ownership and class stratification. The large pieces of property, given over to the leading men of the early days to exploit and develop, still constitute (in spite of important changes and modifications) the basic property pattern. Eighty percent of all fertile land is in the hands of 5-15 percent of the population and in many cases this means a group of interrelated patrician families. The two-class society (lord and servant) still prevails in many Latin American countries, except for the dependent middle-class sectors that modernization has created in a few of them.

The Spanish utopia was never realized. But it did not remain barren. The aftermath of the collision and interaction between the dream of the Christian Kingdom and the actual conditions of the conquest and colonization deserves to be carefully studied.[5] At one end, the inspiration of the dream resulted in a number of laws and regulations which attempted to insure a fair treatment of the Indians and to safeguard their humanity in the process of their evangelization. Most of these laws were in practice either ignored or distorted against their original purpose. A small number of men, nevertheless, particularly missionaries of the religious orders, fought a gallant though losing battle for the enactment of these regulations. Fray Bartolomé de Las Casas has remained in history as the champion of a different colonization and evangelization, one that never took place but which corresponded to the dream of a Christian, "a true way of attracting the Indians to the true religion," as he says in the title of his most important book. Men like him and others are the fountainhead of a small but never interrupted stream of prophetic protest in Latin American Christianity. Revolutionary Christians today can claim their heritage.

A second consequence is historically more important. The relation in Spain between the Church and society—particularly between the Church and the state and the Church and the class structure—was transferred to America. While this meant that the Church had at its disposal all the channels of organized society: legislation, education, access to authority and power, it also meant that it had to pay for it by total and unconditional support of civil authorities. The right of patronage exercised by the king of Spain included the nomination of bishops and even the enforcement of papal decisions in Spanish territories. The Church used the mechanism of civil compulsion, but it depended on the civil authorities and therefore was influenced by their very nature and conditions. When one considers the class

6

organization, which placed in the hands of a few landowning families the total sum of wealth and real authority, it becomes clear that the Church was subordinate, both by its place in the hierarchy of society and by its dependence, to the interests of this group. It is difficult to overestimate the consequences of this fact. It meant that a chasm appeared between the popular—sometimes mixed or syncretistic—religion, which developed among the poor, the Indians, later on the peasants, and the hierarchical structure brought wholesale from Spain. It meant that, while the masses became deeply committed to Catholicism, they always felt the official Church as something foreign to them, as a part of "those above" as popular speech calls the small oligarchy who decides their destiny. It meant, finally, that the Church knew no other way of influencing the people—no other pastoral method—than the use of the institutions of society. This use required a good relation with the dominant classes. This decided their attitudes when the first conflicts began to emerge in Latin American society. The colonial Church was tied to a colonial structure.[6]

A third consequence of the interaction of dream and reality has been less frequently mentioned but is no less important. In spite of individual exceptions (and sometimes unwittingly reinforced and justified by them), there is no doubt that the Christian faith, co-opted into the total Spanish national-religious project, played the role of legitimizing and sacralizing the social and economic structure implanted in America. It served as an ideology to cover and justify existing conditions. God in his Heaven, the king of Spain in his throne, the landlord in his residence: this was "the order of things," God's eternal and sacred order. Class structure and land ownership (and the forms of consciousness corresponding to them) are thus incorporated into the world of sacred representation. As late as 1818, when the movement for emancipation from Spain was sweeping across the continent, the Pope wrote to the Latin American bishops:

> ... as one of the best precepts [of our religion] is that which
> enjoins submission to superior authorities, we do not doubt that in
> the riots that are taking place in those countries ... you will not have
> ceased to inspire your flock with the firm and righteous hatred
> which they must feel toward them.[7]

The Church in its institutional form was part of the Spanish
dream. It was identified with an outmoded and imported order
... and foredoomed to become reactionary when this order
collapsed. The Spanish enterprise—a noble but anachronistic
creation—soon began to disintegrate. British economy and
French Enlightenment, both carried in the holds of the triumphant British navy, and smuggled into Latin America as commerce and books, soon consummated the demise of the Spanish
and Portuguese empires. The "modern" passion for liberty—
free commerce, freedom of thought, religious freedom, individual choice, political emancipation—appealed both to the
minds and to the economic interests of the younger Latin
American "elite," the children of the Spanish colonizers who
saw no reason why the products of their extended estates had
to be monopolized by Spain (while northern Europe promised
better markets) or why authority had to rest on emissaries from
the crown of Spain (when they were the really "significant"
people on the spot). The philosophy of the Enlightenment offered them freedom from the fatalism, passivity, and barren-
ness of Scholastic philosophy and from the narrowness and
rigidity of ecclesiastic morality. Free-tradism broke through
the Spanish monopoly and proclaimed the freedom to open
America to the world. National emancipation was the key to
this new world.

This revolt introduces the second age in our history—the age
of modernization. Our intellectuals conceived it in total opposition to the old colonial order. The Anglo-Saxon world becomes both model and ally in this struggle. "The idea of liberty," wrote the Chilean intellectual Bello, "was a foreign ally
who fought under the banner of emancipation."[8] Sarmiento,

the great liberal teacher and president of Argentina, did not shrink from making the bold contrast:

> Yankee civilization was the product of the plough and the primer; ours was presided by the cross and the sword. There, men learned to work and read, here they learned to idle and to repeat prayers.[9]

The Chilean leader Bilbao summarized the opposition of the old religion and the new world in this either/or: "Either Catholicism or Democracy *(Republicanismo)*."[10]

In the fifty-year-long struggle that ensued between the new liberal leadership and the Roman Catholic Church, several important features of our history took shape. The Church, unprepared for a culture in which it would have to gain its place in society through direct persuasion and influence, naturally sought support in those groups and parties which offered the possibility of extending the traditional forms of influence; it became both dependent on and allied with the conservative parties made up of the rich landowners and the old Spanish aristocracy. It became estranged both from the peasant and emerging workers' classes (who clung to their traditional folk-Catholicism coupled with a profound mistrust and hostility toward the hierarchic Church) and from the intelligentsia who embraced the new philosophical and political ideas. During the first decades of the struggle (1810–1870) a period of great anarchy and confusion left the Church disorganized, without priests, unable to gather around a unifying center and plan. When it recouped, under the direction of Rome, and began to reorganize itself, to train its cadres, to establish its seminaries, to organize lay action, it did so still in the hope of establishing "a new Christendom"—a dream which is not yet altogether dead but which has been shattered by the failure of the Christian Democratic parties to offer a viable alternative in the present revolutionary situation.[11]

But we must get back to the dawn of the modernizing era and

its liberal prophets and leaders. It hardly comes as a surprise that the men engaged in this struggle felt attracted by what they thought were the social, economic, and political consequences of the religion of the Anglo-Saxon countries: Protestantism. They were not so much attracted to it as a personal religion—very few became Protestants themselves. Rather they saw in it, in the first place, an ally in the struggle against clerical domination. Just as emancipation had broken through Spanish commercial monopoly, Protestantism could help to break through Catholic religious monopoly. On the other hand, Protestantism (they referred mostly to Puritanism) had helped to shape the virtues needed for the modern world: freedom of judgment, reliability, a pioneering and enterprising spirit, moral seriousness. It was the religion of activity, culture, and life as opposed to ritualism, idle speculation, and the next world. Under the auspices of these men, conditions were created for the introduction of Protestant missions in Latin America. Religious freedom was insured—not without resistance—and, in some cases, missions or Protestant immigration were sought and invited.

Protestantism came to Latin America in a variety of ways. It was introduced by German, Dutch, and other Protestant immigrant colonies. On the other hand, Anglo-Saxon missions gathered communities of converts around the preaching of a very simple salvation gospel transplanted from the American and British revivals. Educational services were rendered by first-class schools that catered to the liberal elite in the hope of creating a liberal intelligentsia which would change the spiritual atmosphere of the continent. Medical and other services were provided in several places. Protestantism, a proscribed religion in most countries up to 1850, numbered some two hundred thousand by the end of World War I. Later on, it caught on among the restless masses in the form of Pentecostalism, reaching a fantastic total that has already overshot the ten-million mark.[12]

Protestantism entered Latin America between 1870–1890.

Fifty years later, a collection of testimonies gathered among Latin American leading intellectuals documents the understanding of the meaning and function of these churches in the minds of the liberal intelligentsia: [13]

> Among us, *Roman Catholicism has always been incompatible with democracy.* . . . Democracy appeared in our lands as a response to the instinctive cry of popular agony and under the inspiration of Anglo-Saxon democracy. . . . *In the north, democracy was born under the shadow of religion;* here, among us, it appeared in spite of it.

> It does not seem to me that the government of these L.A. Republics should yield to the pressure of Catholic hierarchies for the purpose of obtaining a virtual monopoly. . . . It seems to me that one merchandise that is urgently needed in this land is that of ideas. . . . *It is time that the breezes of the Reformation . . . should blow this way.* Some sections of our countries still struggle along lines of the sixteenth century.

> [The philosophic thought of this country is liberal.] *The presence of Protestant missionaries in Uruguay has created a more favorable attitude toward the U.S.* Why? Because Protestant missionaries understand better than the Catholic ones the principles that are in line with the fundamental democratic spirit of the Uruguayan people.

> Protestantism has given Brazil upright and honest men who have been of great service to our country. *It has awakened in its followers a sense of responsibility* and developed in them *a staunchness of character* that has become a veritable national asset. It has stirred up in its people a hunger to know and given them a taste for reading.

Democracy, freedom, moral uprightness, science, and culture: these are the goals that the new religion is supposed to serve. As one follows the evangelical congresses and the accounts of missionaries, it becomes clear that Protestantism accepted this function. There was, indeed, a great difference between a faith-evangelist, a Presbyterian educator, and a German immigrant. Nevertheless, their conception, implicit or explicit, conscious or unconscious, of the cultural role of Protestantism in Latin

11

America was basically the same. Their creed can be capsuled in a terse sentence from a long-time Presbyterian missionary:

> Christianity, with its emphasis on the worth of the individual and the freedom of the human spirit under the discipline of God is the surest foundation of the liberty and democracy for which Latin America yearns.... That answer can only be given if the evangelical churches are willing to use all their resources and press forward.... [14]

We must forgo, as in the case of Roman Catholicism, a careful consideration of the social, cultural, and religious significance of Protestantism. The main point to be grasped at this moment is the fact that it played a minor but significant role in the liberal-modernistic project that most Latin American countries sought to realize since the middle of the last century. It gave a religious sanction. God was not tied up to the medieval, prescientific, feudal, aristocratic world. He was the God of freedom, culture, democracy, and progress. It is true that in certain ways Protestantism reinforced traditional elements of the culture. But its ethos—even in the more conservative forms—worked in the direction which has been indicated. When a poor peasant or a worker in the new industrial areas becomes a Protestant, he stops drinking, starts working regularly, establishes a stable family, learns to read and write, and consequently gains social and economic status. Quite likely his children will already belong to the "progressive" middle sector of society. Protestantism is thus clearly linked with the whole North Atlantic ideological, cultural, economic, and political thrust beginning with the nineteenth century and up to the present. Protestantism, in terms of its historical origin, of its introduction to Latin America, and of its ethos, came into our world as the religious accompaniment of free enterprise, liberal, capitalist democracy.

Roman Catholicism, clinging with all its forces to the traditional colonial order and its conservative continuation, fought as hard as it could against the introduction of the modern world. But it was, in the end, a self-contradicting stand, because the economic interests of its sponsors became, as the process developed, more and more dependent on the North Atlantic ties. The ideological differences between conservatives and liberals, aristocratic and democratic parties, lost significance in proportion to the unification of their overriding economic concerns. When, since the end of World War I, the masses entered public life, conservatives and liberals became more and more unified around the defense of the capitalist order. The Roman Catholic Church everywhere in the world began at that time a slow march of conversion to the values of modern society. Vatican II was the point of arrival: participatory democracy in the conception and government of the Church, conscious understanding in worship, religious freedom and the dignity of the person as Christian values; and, above all, the defense of the autonomy of culture, science, and the political and economic realms. Some more enlightened Latin American hierarchies (the Chilean one, for instance) had already moved in that direction. Roman Catholicism and Protestantism could, after a long war, join hands in the support of a democratic, enlightened, liberal society in Latin America, a "developed" Latin America which would finally reach the levels of welfare and progress characteristic of the developed North Atlantic community. This was the second and different "Christendom": one, nevertheless, which was destined to be challenged and disrupted before it could even become quite conscious of itself. And we come back here to the beginning of our story and to the "Guevara Christians."

How did the crisis come about? As the process of modernization developed, the darker aspects of the whole "modern enterprise" have begun to loom larger and larger. Latin America suddenly realized that it had been incorporated into the modern world indeed, but not as a junior partner with increasing participation in the total enterprise but as a dependent, serving

13

the further development of the owner's profit. We shall return in the next chapter to the analysis of this process, but we must even now anticipate some basic elements necessary for an understanding of the new Christian consciousness.

The fundamental element in the new Latin American consciousness is the awarness that our political emancipation from Spain was—however justified and necessary—a step in the Anglo-Saxon colonial and neocolonial expansion. Our independence from Spain made us available as suppliers of raw materials first and of cheap labor and manageable markets later on. Two quotations from the British Parliament around 1870 put it crudely: "By maintaining my doctrine of free trade," said one Prime Minister, "I wish to make of England the factory of the world and of America a farm for England." "Argentina," said a legislator, "is our least expensive colony; it even supports its own occupation army."[15] Consequently, our so-called modernization was dictated by the needs and preferences of our overseas masters. The relative diversification and self-sufficiency of an agrarian economy was replaced by a monoculture of those products which were necessary for the metropolis: Argentina was supposed to supply corn and meat; Brazil, coffee; Chile, saltpeter and copper; the Central American countries, bananas; Cuba, sugar; Venezuela, oil, and so on. Railways and roads were built not in order to serve internal or Latin American communications but as a two-beat mechanism in order to pump the production of the country into the large chosen port and to pump it out to the overseas metropolis. The difference between the British and the American phases of the process relate to the different moments of the industrial, technological, and economic history into which their preponderance falls. But the basic fact of the determination of all our economy and development by the needs and problems of the masters prevailing at the time is in all cases the same. The much better known and often condemned political and military interventions, particularly of the United States in Latin America,

14

are only the necessary maneuvers for the protection of this economic relation. *Latin America has discovered the basic fact of its dependence.* This is the real meaning of the liberal-modernistic project.

A second element is the exposure of the "hoax of democracy." It is true that all the forms of democracy were incorporated into our constitutions, but they remained as external to the life of the people as the Spanish "laws of the Indies" had once been. The class structure obtaining at the time of the colonies carried over into the new economic and political conditions. The leaders of the emancipation and modernization had their faces turned toward Europe and the U.S.A. and their backs to the interior of the countries. There, Indians and peasants were simply incorporated as cheap labor for production. Their condition was, if anything, worse than it had been before under a sometimes more or less lenient paternalistic system. A free press, free trade, education, politics—all the "achievements" of liberalism—were the privilege of the elite. For the growing Latin American masses, undernourishment, slavery, illiteracy, and later on forced migration, unemployment, exploitation, crowding, and finally repression when they claim their rights—these are the harvest of one century of "liberal democracy."

The long-range significance of the modernizing project in the history of Latin America is now a moot question. To the writer it seems clear that in time we shall have to recover and incorporate both our colonial and our neocolonial past in our historical consciousness. At that time, we shall see their values and contributions as both negated and transmuted. At the present time, nevertheless, it is most important to realize the gigantic fallacy of the whole modernizing attempt, because the efforts to prolong, consolidate, and carry through this project can only mean greater misery and tragedy for our continent. The basic fallacy consisted in understanding and describing the rise to power and wealth of the North Atlantic countries as a moral achievement due to certain conditions of character and the principles of democracy, free enterprise, and education. Any country, therefore, which would adopt these principles and acquire these qualities would naturally develop in the same way. More recently, technology and planning have been added to the sacred order of development. What was not said or understood was that the rise of the Northern countries took place at a particular moment in history and was built on the possibilities offered by the resources of the dependent countries. Development and underdevelopment are not two independent realities, nor two stages in a continuum but two mutually related processes: Latin American underdevelopment is the dark side of Northern development; Northern development is built on third-world underdevelopment. The basic categories for understanding our history are not development and underdevelopment but domination and dependence. This is the crux of the matter.

We shall return in the next chapter to the analysis of the dynamics of domination and dependence. But, if these things are in any measure true, the liberal ideology under which the liberal project was launched in Latin America, however excellent its intentions may have been, and whatever value it may have had at a point in our history—as a means of breaking the stranglehood of feudal society—proves to be for us *today* an instrument of domination, an ally of neocolonialism and imperialism. This is a conviction growing today among Latin American students, intellectuals, and the masses who reach an awareness of their condition. The rejection of the whole modernizing liberal ideology can come as a result of a socio-economic-political analysis, or simply dawn upon common people as they evaluate their experience at the market, the factory, and the polls. As a matter of fact, liberal ideologists sign the death warrant of their own dreams as they increasingly admit that military governments and an escalation of repression are the only means through which "freedom and democracy" can be "protected." Thus, in the last stage of the process, freedom—the liberal freedom of the modernizers—becomes the ideological justification for a repressive police state. When a person shouts "liberty" in Latin America today, one can immediately suspect him of being a reactionary; and one is seldom wrong.[16]

Christianity faces in Latin America the crisis unleashed by the collapse of the two historical projects to which it had become intimately related. Catholicism suffered the first crisis at the time of the emancipation. To the extent to which it has clung to the old, semifeudal society, it still has this crisis in front of it. This is what Father Gera was referring to when he spoke of the "minority groups, with a position of exasperated reaction prolonging the colonial religio-political monism." "Progressive Catholicism," updated to Vatican II, and Protestantism share the crisis of the modernistic-liberal ideology. Co-opted into the colonial and the neocolonial systems as religious sanction and ideological justification, Christianity faces an agonizing experience of self-criticism.

It is a crisis of conscience, when Christians discover that their churches have become the ideological allies of foreign and national forces that keep the countries in dependence and the people in slavery and need. In a letter to Pope Paul, the Bureau of CLASC (Latin American Committee of Christian Trade Unions, which has some five million Catholic members) expressed this hard judgment at the time of the Eucharistic Congress in 1968:

> Beware, brother Paul. Religion and the Church have constantly been used in Latin America to justify and buttress injustice, oppression, repression, exploitation, persecution, the murder of the poor.[17]

A long history of alliances with the landed aristocracy and their conservative governments, the potential power of the Church, seldom placed at the service of deep changes in society, the contrast of a rich Church and a starving people, these are the food for the crisis so widespread today among Roman Catholic younger priests and laymen, not excluding many bishops.

It is also a crisis of identity, particularly for Protestants. After decades of priding themselves on their progressive stand vis-à-vis Catholicism, they begin to discover that their role was much more ambiguous than they had thought. Even admitting that it was historically necessary to break the power of the traditional colonial mentality, and that Protestantism played a significant role in that respect, they cannot but ask: Did we not, in fact, provide religious sanction to a new colonialism? Did we not in fact contribute to create the benevolent and idealized image of the colonial powers (mainly the U.S.A.) which has disguised the deadly character of their domination? This uneasiness becomes more acute as younger Latin American priests, ministers, and laymen see their churches conforming more and more closely to the reactionary ethos of the oligarchy and the middle classes' alliance with it.

Both Protestants and Catholics, as Father J.-L. Segundo puts it, "suddenly and unexpectedly see their Church serving, in fact, the interests of an inhuman structure."[18] But this "traumatic experience," as he himself calls it, opens the door for a new search—the quest for a post-colonial and a post-neocolonial understanding of the Christian gospel. When Latin American Christians tentatively speak of "a theology of liberation," "a Church of the poor," "the Church of the people," "revolutionary Christianity," and many other expressions which are always quite inadequate and sometimes even misleading, what really is at stake is the urgency to understand what it means to be the People of God in the new Latin America which is painfully emerging. This was the business of Christians for socialism at Santiago, Chile, in 1972. Is there an understanding of Christianity the correlate of which is not dependence but *liberation*?

NOTES

[1] Quoted in "Documento Final," Conclusión.

[2] Lucio Gera, "Apuntes para una interpretación de la Iglesia Argentina," in *Víspera,* no. 15 (Montevideo, 1970) pp. 59 ff. The most comprehensive attempt to write and interpret the history of the Latin American Roman Catholic Church from the point of view of a theology of liberation is that of the historian and philosopher Enrique Dussel in his book *Historia de la Iglesia en América Latina* (Barcelona: Editorial Nova Terra, 1972). The reader interested in historical sources will find in this book the most complete references. In an abbreviated form, Dussel had published his interpretation in *Hipótesis para una historia de la Iglesia en América Latina* (Barcelona: Estela, 1967).

[3] Quoted by John A. Mackay, *The Other Spanish Christ* (London: Student Christian Movement Press, 1932), p. 24.

[4] Ibid., p. 33.

[5] A most perceptive study of this relation, taking Colombia as a case-study, has been published by the sociologist Orlando Fals Borda, *Subversion and Social Change in Colombia* (New York: Columbia University Press, 1969), pp. 36-66.

[6] The best analysis of the sociological and pastoral significance of this relationship has been offered by the North American sociologist Ivan Vallier in his book *Catholicism, Social Control and Modernization in Latin America* (Englewoods Cliffs, N.J.: Prentice-Hall, Inc., 1970), chap. II. Although from a sociological perspective totally opposed to the functionalism of Vallier, the Uruguayan Juan L. Segundo reaches similar conclusions in his book *Pastoral Latinoamericana: sus motivos ocultos* (Buenos Aires: Búsqueda, 1971).

[7] Encyclical "Etsi Longissimo," quoted in Leturia, *Relaciones entre la Santa Sede e Hispanoamérica* (Caracas: Sociedad Bolivariana, 1959), vol. II, pp. 110-113. Even in 1824 the encyclical "Etsi iam diu" speaks of the emancipation movements as "the thistle sowed by the enemy," p. 266; cf. Dussel, *Historia,* p. 110. A good discussion in English of the Church-state relations in Latin America will be found in J. Lloyd Mecham, *Church and State in Latin America* (Chapel Hill: University of North Carolina, 1934).

[8] Andrés Bello, quoted by Leopoldo Zea, *The Latin American Mind* (Oklahoma: University of Oklahoma Press, 1963), p. 51. Both the repudiation of the Spanish heritage and the adoption of the Anglo-American model by the intelligentsia of the time immediately after the emancipation (Bello, Lastarría, Sarmiento, and others) is well documented in this classic book by Zea on the development of the Latin American mind. He also distinguishes very clearly the early liberal trends and the later positivistic ones.

A New Breed of Christians?

⁹ Domingo F. Sarmiento, *Conflicto y armonía de razas en América,* quoted by Zea, *The Latin American Mind,* p. 82.

¹⁰ Francisco Bilbao, quoted by Zea, *The Latin American Mind,* p. 42.

¹¹ Dussel has used the expression "New Christendom" (*Historia,* pp. 124-137) for the desire and the attempts of several sectors in the Roman Catholic Church, between 1930 and 1961, to regain a directive—although rather progressive—role in the Latin American society.

¹² I have tried to develop and document this interpretation of the relation of Protestantism to the Latin American society in the article "Visión del cambio social y sus tareas desde las iglesias cristianas nocatólicas," in the book by Borrat, Comblin, Dussel, et al., *Fe cristiana y cambio social en América Latina* (Salamanca: Sígueme, 1973), pp. 179-203. In a more popular form in the article "The Political Attitude of Protestants in Latin America," translated and published in mimeographed form by James Goff (cf. n. 1 above in the Introduction).

¹³ George P. Howard, *Religious Liberty in Latin America?* (Philadelphia: Westminster Press, 1944). The quotations are, respectively, from M. Alonso Rodríguez, Cuban writer; Enrique Uribe White, Colombian writer; H. Fernández Artucio, Uruguayan legislator; and Manuel C. Ferraz, Brazilian judge. Underlining is ours.

¹⁴ W. Stanley Rycroft, *Religion and Faith in Latin America* (Philadelphia: Westminster Press, 1958), p. 10

¹⁵ Quoted by Gustavo Beyhaut, *Raíces contemporáneas de América Latina* (Buenos Aires: Editorial Eudeba, 1964), p. 40.

¹⁶ Perhaps the most ironic documentation of this fact is the famous Rockfeller Report in which, after a series of prolonged and elaborated visits to Latin America on behalf of President Nixon, Nelson Rockfeller—the "liberal" of American politics and one of the staunchest supporters of the development model for Latin America—comes to the conclusion that strong military governments may be the only way of keeping Latin America free for "democracy" and "progress."

¹⁷ "Carta abierta de trabajadores latinoamericanos al papa Pablo VI," in J.-L. Segundo and R. Cetrulo (eds.) *Iglesia Latinoamericana, ¿protesta o profecía?* (Buenos Aires: Ediciones Búsqueda, 1969), p. 82.

¹⁸ Juan L. Segundo, *De la sociedad a la teología* (Buenos Aires: Editorial Carlos Lohlé, 1970), p. 150.

Chapter Two

Understanding
Our World

"Because the decade of *developmentalism* is over and we are now inaugurating the decade of *liberation.* Because liberation is the new name of development." In these words the editor prefaces a collection of essays on the theology of liberation in Latin America.[1] As a matter of fact, the articulation of their obedience and the account of their faith are, for the Christians of whom we are now reporting, premised by this conviction. It rests on an analysis and interpretation of the Latin American situation for which the transition from developmentalism (or reformism) to liberation is crucial. Their action and their reflection are of such a nature that they make no sense outside of such an analysis. If it is wrong, they are proved wrong. An engaged faith and obedience cannot stand outside or above the world in which they are engaged. This is the reason why, in the effort to enter into this theology, we are forced to dwell on the understanding and analysis of the world in which it finds its *locus.*

There is, in the first place, an awareness of the situation in which people are living in our continent. There is here no theory or interpretation but simple experience, open to anyone who is willing to visit Latin America and move a few blocks away from the central hotels. The Santiago meeting put it in these terms:

> The socioeconomic, political, and cultural situation of the Latin American peoples challenges our Christian conscience. Unemploy-

21

ment, malnutrition, alcoholism, infant mortality, illiteracy, prostitution, an ever-increasing inequality between the rich and the poor, racial and cultural discrimination, exploitation, and so forth are facts that define a situation of institutionalized violence in Latin America.[2]

An Argentine bishop, Alberto Devoto, in a recent pastoral letter, describes the situation:

Factors many times mentioned keep their actuality: a growing rate of unemployment, a constant increase of the cost of living, inadequate health provision, the desperate situation of rural families, never fulfilled official promises, the boom of corruption and gambling, the lack of freedom of expression, varied forms of violence, repressive legislation calculated to intimidate the people, the lack of participation of the people in decisions, etc. . . . If anything, all these problems are escalating at a frightening speed.[3]

These are impressionistic pictures of the situation. They can easily be translated into the cold language of figures and statistics. Here are a few facts extracted from a United Nations' report of a few years back:

• Two-thirds, if not more, of the Latin American population are physically undernourished to the point of starvation in some regions [coca-chewing, alcohol, even mud-eating in some areas are attempts at compensation].

• Three-fourths of the population in several of the Latin American countries are illiterate; in the others, from 20 to 60 percent. [In relatively advanced countries like Argentina, illiteracy and school desertion have increased in the last ten years; Cuba has practically eliminated illiteracy and Chile was on the way to doing so.]

• One-half of the Latin American population are suffering from infectious or deficiency diseases. [While "degenerative" or "deterioration" diseases account for 48.7 percent of deaths in the U.S.A., they occupy a modest 7-10 percent in Latin America; people do not live there long enough to worry about cancer or heart failure.]

• About one-third of the Latin American working population [particularly the great majority of the millions of Indian laborers] continue to remain outside the economic, social, and cultural pale of the Latin American community. The consuming power of the Latin American Indian is in many areas almost nil. . . .

• An overwhelming majority of the Latin American agricultural population is landless. Two-thirds, if not more, of the agricultural, forest, and livestock resources of Latin America are owned or controlled by a handful of native landlords and foreign corporations. [In the recently opened Amazonia, in Brazil, sixty million acres have been bought by U.S.A. investors in the last five years.]

• Most of the extractive industries in Latin America are owned or controlled by foreign corporate investment, a considerable portion of the profits being taken out of the various countries. In like fashion, many of the institutions of production and distribution in Latin America are controlled by absentee foreign capital [American investment in L.A. between 1950-65 adds up to 3.8 billion dollars; benefits transferred to U.S.A. in that period 11.3 billion; deducting foreign aid in that period there is a net 5 billion dollars favorable to U.S.A. Lately also most banks and financial institutions in many countries have been bought by foreign banks.]

• Living conditions for the bulk of the Latin American population are particularly unstable, being dependent on the fluctuations of the foreign market. Concentration on one extractive industry or on monocultural production . . . for foreign consumption . . . has brought many areas to the verge of economic ruin. [The last dramatic example is the economic shipwreck of Uruguay with the fall of the wool market due to the production of synthetic materials.]

• Intra- and inter-Latin American trade is largely undeveloped. . . .

• Except for Colombia, Argentina, Brazil, and Uruguay, the percentage of "active" or gainfully employed people is considerably lower in Latin America than in the U.S.A. and on the European continent (40.8 percent in U.S.A.; 45 percent in Europe; 43 percent in Australia; 30 percent in Latin America). [Unemployment has climbed in Brazil, Uruguay, and Argentina in the last five years.][4]

Data is abundant and telling. The picture the figures depict is impressive. Few would deny it. Hardly anyone would claim that such conditions are acceptable. The ways part, nevertheless, concerning the diagnosis of the origin and cure for these evils. In this context is the contrast between the developmentalists (or reformists) and the revolutionaries.

Around 1950 a great hope was roused by the plans for development. Latin America (as indeed all the third world) were, according to this interpretation, still in the earlier stages of a process of development which, in the Northern world had already been achieved. We were still immersed in traditional society: our economies were unplanned and did not incorporate all the population in the chain of production; our dependence on extractive industries (agriculture, cattle raising, mines) placed us at the mercy of world markets both for the export of raw materials and the acquisition of manufactured goods, thus creating unfavorable terms of trade. At the same time, a static mentality, still tied to the land, to conservation, to the rhythm of nature, crippled us, preventing the domination of nature which is necessary for development. This was the basic diagnosis. How could the situation be changed? The economy had to be planned and integrated; production, diversified; industrialization, accelerated; health and education, raised to an acceptable level; marginal population, incorporated in the national life and the productive process.

How was this to be achieved? In the Northern world, it was said, this had already been done. The key was the accumulation of capital and the introduction of technology and planning. If these movements could be accelerated, a "takeoff point" would arrive, after which our economies would expand naturally and the welfare and consumer society already present in the Northern world would also appear in our horizon. For this purpose, Latin American countries had to organize themselves internally, stabilize their economy, avoid political unrest, effect certain basic reforms in land tenure and taxation in order to redistribute wealth in a more efficient way and offer attractive conditions to "first world" investment which would introduce the necessary capital and technology.

The U.N. proclaimed the first "decade for development" in

1950. A number of international organizations were created: the International Development Bank (IDB), International Aid for Development (AID), International Monetary Fund (IMF), and others. The countries of the third world met at Bandung (1955) in order to strive together for better terms of trade. The U.N. created an organization for this purpose, the United Nations Commission for Trade and Development (UNCTAD), and an Economic Committee for Latin America (CEPAL). Populist governments appeared in several Latin American countries. Some Latin American countries seemed to be in optimum conditions, on the verge of reaching the takeoff point: Argentina, Mexico, Chile, Venezuela, Brazil. John Kennedy launched, in the midst of great expectations, the Alliance for Progress in 1961.

Soon after the launching of the Alliance for Progress, the failure was already visible. The chasm between the developed and the underdeveloped world was growing wider instead of narrowing, not only because the expected minimum measure of growth was never reached, but because, applied to widely different starting points, even the same rate of growth results in ever increasing inequality. Foreign investment has taken out of Latin America far more than it has invested. The process of production, distribution, and finance has been almost totally transferred to outside agents (international monopolies). The terms of trade continue to be unfavorable. The prices paid for the use of technology—protected by licenses in the Northern world—far outweighs the benefits of its use. Production has been unable to cope with the increase of population and thus the number and condition of marginals have become worse. No major reform in land tenure or distribution of wealth has taken place except in Cuba, Chile, and Peru. Consequently, social unrest is rampant on the continent, and populist regimes have been replaced, with the aid and support of the U.S.A., by military, repressive governments which can guarantee the stable conditions required by foreign investment.

Is this failure merely accidental? Is it due to inability on the part of the Latin Americans or to bad faith on the part of the Northern world? Could it be corrected with greater skill, better intentions, a longer time, and harder work? It is possible to find all kinds of qualifications. For a growing number of Latin Americans, nevertheless, the reason for the failure lies deeper, in the very nature of the economic system. The Christians meeting in Santiago expressed it in this way. "This unjust society has its objective basis in the capitalist relations of production that necessarily generate a class society."[5] Is this merely an ideological dogma or is it the result of a sober analysis of what has taken place in Latin America and is still taking place here? We shall recapitulate very briefly some of the basic elements in this analysis.[6]

The theory of development which was applied to the third world rests on an unhistorical and mechanistic analysis (dependent on functionalist sociology) which makes at least three fundamental mistakes. The first is to believe that history is unilinear and that a society can move to previous stages of other existing societies. As a matter of fact, all societies move in a parallel and interrelated way. The "takeoff point" in Northern societies was dependent on the relation to the then colonized societies. That situation does not obtain today and the process therefore cannot be repeated. Secondly, the model did not take into account the political factors: there is an "effect of demonstration" which moves the masses to demand participation in wealth and welfare, and therefore the "slave labor" that was available in the early stages of the developed societies cannot be obtained today—hence social unrest and repression. Thirdly, the theory took for granted that the developed countries were the "normal" model for the underdeveloped. As the process continues, the third world becomes less and less attracted by the quality of life and the nature of the North Atlantic societies.

When we realize that development and underdevelopment

are not two successive stages in an abstract and mechanical process but two dimensions of one single historical movement, it becomes evident that Latin America has to be studied as the *dependent* or dominated part in that process. This realization has given birth to a new form or analysis: the study of dependent societies. This is a major scientific achievement in Latin American sociology. Dependence can be defined as:

> . . . the situation in which the economy of one group of countries is conditioned by the development and expansion of another economy. The interrelationship . . . assumes the form of dependence when some countries (the dominant ones) are able to develop themselves while others (the dependent ones) can only reflect that expansion.[7]

Roman Catholic bishops meeting at Medellín in 1968 put it in less technical language:

> We refer here to the consequences of the dependence of our countries from a center of economic power around which they gravitate. From this it results that our nations are not masters of their own resources and economic decisions. Obviously, this is not without effects on the political realm.[8]

This dependence is not a new fact; the Latin American countries came into "universal" history (the history of the West) as dependent entities under the Spanish colonization, and were assigned a place in that world: that of providing resources for Spain (mainly gold and silver, then some agricultural products) in the trade-capitalism which then predominated. When capitalism developed in the Northern nations into other stages: industrial and then consumer capitalism, the role of the dependent nations also changed: they were destined to provide raw materials and agricultural products first and cheap labor and markets later.

When developmentalists claim that the capitalist system is by nature dynamic and progressive, they do not realize that, while it has indeed been so for the Northern countries, it does not necessarily mean it will be so for the dependent countries. In fact, this is not the case. An expert from the Inter-American Development Bank explained not long ago:

> Investment is capital-intensive. To the extent that private capital contributes to economic growth, assuming that no deliberate effort is made to turn society upside down, *it will not provide significant places for the marginal masses in the system.*[9]

The truth of this assertion is dramatically illustrated by Brazil. For the last seven years that country has applied relentlessly a development model, massively supported by American investment and the U.S. government. Brazil is evidently bent on creating a showpiece and a subordinate center of power in the Latin American continent. Political and police repression has been applied with cold and absolute brutality in order to avoid any unrest which might interfere with economic growth. An intensive propaganda has been launched in order to create "a mentality of development," a sense of greatness and destiny. After seven years, the Brazilian government can boast of one of the highest rates of growth of the gross national product. What is not told is that 41. 6 percent of the total Brazilian industry is in foreign hands (94 percent in the chemical industry, 100 percent in the automotive industry, 82 percent in the rubber industry, and 71 percent in railways). The purchasing value of the salary has fallen 23.5 percent. The repatriation of profits to the centers of investment has multiplied in four years (1964–1968) by 4.2 percent and keeps increasing. The naked truth is that Brazil has become, not even a colony of a foreign power, but a factory of multinational corporations; the Brazilian population, a reserve of cheap labor, and the Brazilian government, army, and police, foremen and wardens of these corporations.[10]

There is scarcely any need to dwell on the political and military power which the Northern countries, mainly the

U.S.A. use to support their economic interests. Any country which attempts to escape economic occupation immediately faces a whole series of sanctions (the Hickenlooper Amendment, U.S. vote against loans by the IMF, the IDB, or other international agencies to countries which have nationalized American interests, reduction in import quotas, and finally economic blockade). This is immediately reinforced by concerted campaigns by the press. Finally, as direct military intervention—like in Santo Domingo in 1962—becomes inconvenient, there is support by ITT, American agencies like CIA, and even the State Department to local military coups which might restore conditions favorable to American investment. Recent history in relation to Cuba, Peru, and Chile and the reactionary coup in Bolivia (in which Brazil played the role of sub-imperial station) amply document these facts. On the other hand, CIA support of local police intelligence and Pentagon aid to armies in neofascist Latin American regimes serve as preventive measures for the same purpose.

In describing all of this, we must avoid moral indignation clouding the nature of the issue. We are not dealing with particularly wicked people or with cancerous outgrowths of a system which has to be cleansed and restored to health. We are simply facing the normal and unavoidable consequences of the basic principles of capitalist production as they work themselves out in our global, technological time. The concentration of economic power, the search for higher profits, the efforts to obtain cheaper labor and to avoid higher costs are of the very essence of that system. When theoreticians of neocapitalism in the developed countries point out that the most cruel consequences of these principles have been eliminated in the Northern nations, they usually pay insufficient attention to the fact that these changes have been obtained through conflict and that they have been made possible by the discovery and exploitation of another proletariat, that of the third world.

It would be seriously misleading to describe the relation of

29

dependence as a purely external matter, a relation obtaining between two separate and global entities. The truth is that Northern and peripheral countries, or dominating and dependent countries are part of a single history, mutually determine each other's internal structures and relationships, culture and styles of living. From the point of view of the dependent countries, this phenomenon has been called "the internalization of dependence." Several aspects must be mentioned in this connection. The most important has to do with class structure in the dependent countries. Foreign economic interests reinforced in early stages (and still do in certain areas) the traditional two-class society, tying the higher class (land- and plantation-owners, cattle raisers) to foreign markets and inducing a standard of living available through the import of culture and manufactured goods, thus developing highly sophisticated foreign-oriented islands in the colonized world. More important, these interests created in time a new economic elite for the exploitation and administration of extractive industries and the management and distribution of consumer industries. In this way, social groups appeared whose interests are totally dependent on those of the foreign concerns. Lately, conscious efforts have been made to co-opt some of the higher echelons of these groups as directly as possible into the multinational corporations through buying decisive stock in local capital and including some of these people—and, very significantly, higher military officers—in local directories of subsidiary foreign companies. Frequent visits to and training courses in the Northern countries for economic and military agents strengthen the homogeneity of procedure, viewpoint, and ideology. Local bourgeoisie in the dependent countries reach an almost total solidarity with foreign interests.

Cultural penetration completes this picture. Mass media, owned in some cases by foreign concerns and dependent in all on international news agencies, film and record production, and many other elements, spread even to the far corners of the third world the values and ideology of the Northern countries. Anti-communist and pro-Western ideological indoctrination and a systematic hallowing of the "Western capitalist style of life" pervade almost everything that the common man reads, listens to, or looks at every day. Massive propaganda of consumer goods shapes the tastes and creates artificial needs. The use of sports for mass consumption and lately legalized and propagandized gambling reinforce this culture of alienation. Through all these means critical awareness is killed, and a society which ought to be motivated for effort and solidarity is led to escape from reality and to develop the habits and concerns of a leisure- and consumption-oriented world.

In the final analysis, the capitalist form of production as it functions in today's world creates in the dependent countries (perhaps not only in them) a form of human existence characterized by artificiality, selfishness, the inhuman and dehumanizing pursuit of success measured in terms of prestige and money, and the resignation of responsibility for the world and for one's neighbor. This last point is perhaps the most serious. Insofar as this sham culture kills in the people even the awareness of their own condition of dependence and exploitation, it destroys the very core of their humanity: the decision to stand up and become agents of their own history, the will to conceive and realize an authentic historical project.

The process we have analyzed, nevertheless, develops at the same time its own internal contradictions, in and through which dependent men and society claim their humanity and begin a struggle for liberation. These contradictions are the point of departure for a new consciousness, which is growing in our continent. There is, at a very simple level, the contradiction created by the "effect of demonstration"—the desire for, indeed the subjective need of, the goods produced by the consumer industry coupled with the deteriorating standard of living. The revolution of rising expectations, as it has been called, creates a sense of frustration and rebellion in the growing marginal and semimarginal populations. Moreover, in an economy subject to permanent inflation, the urban *petit bourgeoisie* (small house industry, liberal professionals) and white-collar workers suffer in a particularly acute way this contradiction between high expectations and the deteriorating purchasing power of their income. It is not strange that in the recent popular riots in some major Argentine cities (Córdoba, Mendoza, Rosario, Tucumán) during the time of the military government (1968-1969) the middle class found itself spontaneously joining the workers in setting fire to foreign concerns, breaking the windows of the large stores, and erecting barricades against the police.

Another contradiction develops between local middle and small industry (non-monopolistic) and the monopolies. The former finds itself more and more asphyxiated under the growing power of the latter, which monopolizes private and public credit, reduces costs of production, controls the market and prices them out of it at their will. Thus, at certain moments, and at least temporarily, these groups become allies of the workers in the struggle against foreign imperialism. In order to assess the importance of this element, we see significantly that in a country like Chile, for instance, small and middle capital constitutes 97 percent of the total industry, but uses only 56 percent of the total labor force and owns 42 percent of the total capital investment. With due changes, a similar analysis can be made of small and middle rural production in relation to large landowners and rural corporations.

At the ideological level, these contradictions take the form of and lend force to a very important conflict: the mounting reaction of younger people, students, and groups of professionals (teachers, professors, lawyers, architects, etc.) against the conception of life and the values and attitudes of capitalist society. The values of justice and human dignity inherent in the Christian tradition, in the face of the widespread misery and suffering which the system is creating, awaken a reaction of pain and anger. When foreign interests and their local clientele resort to repression, persecution, torture, and cold-blooded murder in order to protect their interests, a sense of national dignity, of human solidarity, of elemental justice sends these people to the struggle.[11]

Basic to all of this, of course, is the fundamental contradiction between the capitalist form of production and the worker whose labor is exploited. Labor has been organized in the major Latin American countries for more than a half century. It has a varied and complex history into which we cannot enter at the moment. The important thing to point out is that organized labor is slowly bursting the straitjacket of the purely vindicative, nonpolitical role into which the capitalist state has tried to force it. In country after country (Chile, Uruguay, Argentina), it realizes that the struggle for better conditions leads inevitably to the political arena and to the question of power. Thus, the workers slowly enter into the revolutionary inheritance which is their own.

In this brief picture of the awakening of a revolutionary consciousness in Latin America a crucial date must be mentioned: 1958. The triumph of the Cuban revolution marks a new time in Latin America. It indicates that the capitalist and imperialist system can be overcome, even at a scanty seventy miles from the U.S.A. and against the concerted effort of it and its satellites. In the seventeen years that have elapsed we have learned that Castro's way of access to power cannot be copied everywhere, that the Cuban revolution is not a model to be reproduced. But it remains as a sign that change is possible, however costly. An inroad has been opened in a system that must be subverted and changed. The hypocritical denunciation that Cuba has been "exporting" and financing" revolution in the continent, frequently voiced by those who are actively engaged in exporting and financing repression, is certainly exaggerated. But it is true that Cuba has been the cradle of a new revolutionary consciousness in these lands.

We have thus far summarized the basic analysis of the Latin American situation which underlies the position that the Christians for socialism (in their diverse forms and groups) have taken. It would be necessary to add a number of qualifications in order to do justice to the immense work which is being done. On the other hand, there are differences of interpretation at many points, and in some a fierce discussion. The difference between the populist tendencies which emphasize the concept of "people" over against that of "classes" and the classic Marxist approach, the debate over the revolutionary significance of a concentration on the struggle against imperialism as a stage in the road to socialism, the relative importance given to violent subversion over against the use of constitutional means, are not easy problems. It is not difficult to detect the Marxist frame of reference implicit in this diagnosis of the Latin American situation. In the second part of our work we shall have to discuss the theological significance and the problems raised by this appropriation of Marxist categories.[12] At this point we can confine ourselves to a few brief comments concerning the use of this methodology of analysis.

The first has to do with its objectivity. Sociologists belonging to functionalist and structuralist schools frequently denounce the "partisanship" of this analysis. The simple fact is that the evident and concrete failure of the developmentalist and reformist plans has unmasked the partisanship of the liberal (functionalist) sociology. It has made crystal clear that, insofar as it borrowed its categories from the bourgeois society and interpreted all phenomena in the third world in those categories, it was actually taking that society for granted as a norm and, to that extent, denying history and confining change to modifications within the system. Far from being objective and nonpartisan, it was reactionary, an "underdeveloping sociology" as someone called it. It became clear also that such a neutral science of society does not exist. Marxism, on the other hand, offered a framework of study open to the dynamism of history and to a projective view of human activity. Its conflictive understanding of reality was truer to our situation. In this sense it is more objective than a supposedly neutral science which is in fact unavowedly committed to the preservation of the status quo.

But, for the same reason, a rigid Marxist orthodoxy or dogmatism is immediately rejected. Class structure, for instance, has to be studied in terms of the realities given in a dependent country, while Marx and Lenin had analyzed it as it appeared in the Northern countries. The forms of monopolistic, multinational capitalism, again, require a rethinking of classical formulations. The relation of superstructural instances (culture, religion) to the struggle for liberation has to be reassessed. The Marxist scheme cannot be taken as a dogma but rather as a method which has to be applied to our own reality in terms of this reality, and this in turn reverts to a reconsideration of the method itself. Just as the socialist system which will finally emerge in the Latin American countries will not be a copy of the existing ones, but a creation related to our reality, so the analysis has to be adequate to this reality and develop its own categories and methods.

Such new categories and methods are, moreover, not developed in abstraction or in pure objective contemplation, but in the very effort to overcome the present situation and move forward to a new society. The analysis which is required, therefore, is to some extent anticipatory. It has to project reality as well as to dissect it. Otherwise it merely reinforces the present situation and, to that extent, it falsifies the movement of history and misses the most important dimension of reality. But such an anticipatory science requires commitment to a historical project, which, in turn, is born of a certain discernment of the future. To put it in theological terms, it demands a form of prophecy. Here we touch the delicate relation between science and ideology and ideology and utopia, to which we shall have to return in later chapters. The important point here is to realize the unavoidable relation between analysis and commitment. The Christian revolutionary commitment which we shall try to present in the next chapter is certainly based on the analysis sketched in the present one. But this analysis is also made in the context of that commitment. And this is not a vicious but a creative circle, in fact the only possibility for analysis to be a human—i.e., a projective—science and for commitment to be a human—i.e., a rational—commitment.

NOTES

[1] Gustavo Pérez (ed.), *Simposio sobre Teología de la Liberación* (Bogotá: Editorial Presencia, 1970), vol. II, p. 4. There is an English translation: "Theology of Liberation: Bogotá, 1970," in *IDOC-NA,* no. 14 (New York, November 28, 1970), pp. 66 ff.

[2] "Documento Final," part I, 1.1.

[3] Mons. Alberto Devoto, "Pautas para una reflexión de la Iglesia de Goya al comenzar el año 1973," in *La Opinión* (Buenos Aires, February 13, 1973), p. 8.

[4] United Nations, *Informe preliminar sobre la situación social del Mundo* (New York: U.N. Publications, 1952). Comments in brackets are by the author. Recent data can be found in United Nations' reports. A good summary, giving balanced and even conservative figures and sources, will be found in J. de Santa Ana, "La insatisfacción de las masas en América Latina," *Cristianismo y Sociedad,* año II, no. 5 (Montevideo, 1964), pp. 26-35.

[5] "Documento Final," part I, 1.4.

[6] It is impossible to indicate here the immense amount of sociological, economic, and cultural research that has taken place in Latin America during the last fifteen years, offering an analysis of the "situation of dependence." We could not exaggerate the importance of this work, even in relation to the emergence of a "theology of liberation." There is a good summary and numerous bibliographical references in Gustavo Gutiérrez, *A Theology of Liberation* (Maryknoll, N.Y.; Orbis Books, 1971), pp. 81-99. Another excellent summary is the article by Gonzalo Arroyo, "Pensamiento latinoamericano sobre subdesarrollo y dependencia externa," in Borrat, Comblin, Dussel, et al. *Fe cristiana y cambio social en América Latina,* pp. 319 ff. A number of the most distinguished scholars in this area (Celso Furtado, Theotonio dos Santos, R. Stavenhagen, F. H. Cardoso) have contributed to the collection edited by Henry Bernstein, *Underdevelopment and Development: The Third World Today* (Middlesex, England: Penguin Books, 1973).

[7] T. dos Santos, "La crisis de la teoría del desarrollo y las relaciones de dependencia en América Latina," in *La dependencia político-económica de América Latina* (Mexico D.F.: Siglo Veintiuno, 1969), p. 180.

[8] C.E.L.A.M., "Segunda Conferencia General del Episcopado Latinoamericano," *La Iglesia en la actual transformación de América Latina a la luz del Concilio* (Bogotá: Publicaciones de la Conferencia Episcopal Latinoamericana, 1968), 2 vols.; Sección "Paz," par. 8. There is an English version in *Between Honesty and Hope* (Maryknoll, N.Y.: Maryknoll Documentation Series, 1970), p. 203.

[9] Jerome I. Levinson, of the Inter-American Development Bank, in the minutes of the "Council on Foreign Relations" (a group of financial experts and investors in Latin America, sponsored by David Rockefeller), *NACLA's Latin American and Empire Report*, vol. V, no. 7 (November, 1971), p. 13.

[10] Among the numerous writings dealing with the "Brazilian model" we single out the recent excellent book by Fernando Enrique Cardoso, *O Modelo Político Brasileiro* (Sao Paulo: Difusão Europeia do Livro, 1973), including several statistical tables. The data in the text has been taken from a series of research articles on Brazil in the Argentine paper in Buenos Aires, *La Opinion,* "El costo político del modelo económico brasileño" (February 21, 1973, p. 15 and February 22, 1973, p. 13) and "El costo social del modelo económico brasileño" (February 25, 1973, p. 11 and February 27, 1973, p. 19).

[11] It is important to point out that these same concerns and attitudes are gaining ground in some sectors of the armies, particularly among younger officers. The Peruvian, semi-socialist regime is the first point at which this new form of military intervention has come to power. But this is not the only place where it is at work.

[12] I am attempting a more systematic discussion of the relation of the Christian faith to Marxism in the context of the common participation in the struggle for liberation in the "London Lectures on Contemporary Christianity," to be published by Hodder and Stoughton (London) in 1975.

Chapter Three

The Awakening
of the
Christian Conscience

"The peasant has never got a fair deal. And never will so long as capitalism exists," spontaneously answers a Mexican *campesino* when asked about possible solutions for the problems of cultivating and selling his tomatoes. "For a socialist Argentina," shout the young Peronists as the time of election approaches. "Even a blind person can see that Latin America moves irreversibly toward some form of socialism," declares Bishop Antulio Parrilla Bonilla from Puerto Rico. These are not testimonies of doctrinaire Marxists or sophisticated political analysts. They are—whether true or not—the expression of a conviction which (with celebration or regret) is gaining ground in the consciousness of the Latin American people. One way to express it would be to say that, reaching back to deep-rooted moments and trends in our history, but gaining strength and precision in the last ten or fifteen years, a "historical project" is afoot in Latin America, which gradually mobilizes the imagination, the resources, and the will of the younger Latin American generations.

"Historical project" is an expression frequently used in our discussions as a midway term between an utopia, a vision which makes no attempt to connect itself historically to the present, and a program, a technically developed model for the organization of society. A historical project is defined enough to force options in terms of the basic structures of society. It points in a given direction. But frequently its contents are expressed in symbolical and elusive forms rather than in terms of precise technical language. For this reason a single historical project may cover a number of different and even conflicting views concerning technical aspects or tactical conception.[1] It is in this general sense that we speak of *a Latin American socialist project of liberation.*

In spite of the imprecision, certain basic elements constitutive of the project can be singled out: (1) It rejects the "developmentalist" attempt to solve the Latin American problems within the capitalist international system, depending on the relations to the Northern countries; instead it envisages a breaking away from the domination of the "empires"—though not necessarily an isolation from them. (2) It is convinced that such elimination of dependence is impossible without a *parallel* revolution in the social structure of Latin American societies, through which the oligarchic elites which cooperate with foreign interests are displaced from power; this is only possible through a mobilization of the people (there are here differences as to the relative weight of the peasants and industrial proletariat, the role of the military and of the revolutionary elite, and a possible first step in which local nondependent groups of the bourgeoisie may collaborate). (3) Given the well-experienced reaction of foreign and local interests to such a program, the need for nationalizations, etc., it is clear that a strong centralized state is a necessary step in the process; (this does not mean a naive attitude concerning the dangers of such a step). (4) It is not enough to bring about changes in the economic structure of society: they must be accompanied, supported, and carried out by the awakening of a sense of participation in the population (particularly in the oppressed people), whereby they become true protagonists of their own history (again, there are different forms of conceiving this *conscientization* or *politicization,* but in all cases there is a strong emphasis on the cultural dimension).[2] (5) Given the fact that a transfer of power is necessary, which implies a clear consciousness of the objectives involved, a sense of urgency and concentration, and a serious and prolonged struggle, the political dimension becomes primary and determinant; other important aspects (technical, cultural, social, economic) become subordinate, not in the sense of neglect or subestimation but in that of relationship to the political; hence we speak of a primacy of the political in the present Latin American struggle. (6) There is a strong sense of the freedom to find an authentic Latin American socialism, forged in a realistic understanding of our situation, true to our own history and to the characteristics of the Latin American people; in this sense there is a strong rejection of Marxist (or any other) dogmatism, however indebted we are to its analysis and participation, and a refusal to accept any one of the existing models (even Cuba) as a stereotype to be copied. (While socialism is a common feature, the amount of "heterodoxy" in socialist terms varies greatly all the way from the Peronist "third way" to the Peruvian socializing military regime, to the "constitutional road to socialism" in Chile, to the communist Moscow- or Peking-type parties). (7) Development is not seen as merely economic or structural change; rather, there is a strong emphasis on the human dimension. A Marxist revolutionary like Guevara and Christians like Dom Helder Cámara or Camilo Torres are at one on this point: liberation is the process through which and in which a "new man" must emerge, a man shaped by solidarity and creativity over against the individualistic, distorted humanity of the present system.[3]

It is beyond the scope of our work to discuss the nature, program, and strategies of the different groups working in Latin America for the project we have tried to characterize. It is, nevertheless, important to bear in mind the plurality and diversity. *Foquismo* (small groups of guerrillas operating in the interior of the countries and serving as "centers of irradiation" for a revolutionary participation of the people) is still alive but has proved questionable in the light of Guevara's (and recently of Caamaño's) experience in Bolivia (and Santo Domingo). The mobilization for "a popular uprising" and the takeover of power requires a serious and extended work of politicization of the masses, helping them to become aware of the contradictions of the system under which they suffer. At the same time, the brutal, thoroughgoing, and organized repression which such work of "conscientization" and politicization meets in several countries has led some to conceive of a transitional phase in which a restricted change in coalition with military or national capitalist groups opposed to imperialism may offer an opening for a socialist society. Finally, in some countries (as formerly in Chile, possibly Uruguay) there was a hope that power might be achieved through constitutional means. There are variations in all these possibilities. There is also fierce controversy and denunciation among them. In fact, the atomization of the left is one of the serious problems confronting Latin American revolutionaries. But there is no doubt as to the mounting response to the historical project which, as a totality, they represent. This is the background against which we must see the existence of "revolutionary Christians."

"Christians, urged on by the spirit of the gospel"—writes the Santiago *Document*—"are joining the proletarian groups and parties without asking for any rights or duties different from those of any other revolutionary." "The Latin American process"—the *Document* says at another point—"is a single and global process. Christians neither have nor want to have a political road of their own."[4] The participation of Christians in the revolutionary struggle is not merely an aspiration: it is a simple fact. Among the guerrillas, in the political parties, in the shanty towns, in the university, among the peasants—wherever the revolutionary ferment is at work, there are Christians, Catholic and Protestant alike, working shoulder to shoulder with other men. They are found in jail, among the tortured and murdered, with the persecuted and exiled. And, when some

41

measure of success is achieved, they are there with the others working for the creation of a new society and a new man.

> The point of departure of our theological reflection [writes the Peruvian theologian G. Gutiérrez] is the process of liberation in Latin America. More concretely, it is the engagement in this process which Latin Americans are assuming. Even more precisely: it is the engagement of Christians in the process of liberation. This I would call the *major fact* in the life of the Latin American Church in recent times.[5]

This is not simply a statement made by Christians in order to boost their "rating" in a revolutionary world. It is a fact openly recognized everywhere in the subcontinent. Conservative governments, classes, and ideologists see it with surprise and dismay, as they realize the danger of losing the support of a longtime ally in the struggle to maintain the status quo. Revolutionaries greet it also with surprise and joy, welcoming their participation, without being able to understand this phenomenon which runs counter to all their theories about the role of religions and religious people! And some begin to suspect that there may be a deeper and hidden connection between the Christian faith and revolutionary change. None less than Fidel Castro, an avowed Marxist-Leninist, has devoted several paragraphs in recent speeches to the recognition and assessment of this "new fact."

> Now then. During the last years, revolutionary trends have been appearing among the Christians in Latin America. Or, if you prefer, progressive trends which drift toward revolutionary positions. There is a great number of priests and religious people who take a definite stand in favor of the process of liberation in Latin America. . . . Some are persecuted, others have died, like Camilo Torres. In fact, if we analyze things objectively . . . we must appreciate in its full value the importance of this awakening of a political consciousness of large masses of Christians in this continent. . . .
> We had many things to talk about with "the Christian left" . . .

many things which are not the result of opportunism but of convictions, not the result of seeking advantages but of deep reasons, of principles. . . .[6]

We must now make an effort to trace some of the moments and characteristics of this new Christian revolutionary consciousness as it has appeared in Latin America. We shall first look at two pioneers. Then we shall try to suggest something of the spread of the movement. Finally we shall briefly characterize some organized movements.

In the little town of El Carmen, Colombia, on Tuesday the 15th of February, 1966, Camilo Torres, the priest turned guerrilla, was ambushed and killed. The news flashed like lightning throughout Latin America. Was Torres an apostate? Couldn't he have chosen a different road without betraying his vocation? Was he lured by a romantic illusion into forgetting his specific task as priest? A study of his career—his itinerary to revolutionary violence—provides an excellent case study of the situation, the options, the pitfalls and the risks for a Christian who becomes aware of the condition in which his people live and tries to respond actively to it. "I am a revolutionary," said Torres, "because I am priest."[7]

Born of a wealthy and aristocratic stock and destined to become a lawyer, Camilo felt the call to the priesthood as a call to service: "I was chosen by Christ to be eternally a priest, moved by the desire to give myself full-time to love my neighbors." After completing with honors his theological studies, he was sent to Louvain for special training in sociology. Back in Colombia, as teacher and chaplain at the National University, he began to analyze the national situation and to articulate for himself and for his students the results of his analysis. He believed that to be a Christian is to care for men in their concrete, particular needs. He asked that the traditional order of priorities of the Catholic Church in Latin America be revised: "In my view, the hierarchy of priorities should be reversed: love, the teaching of doctrine, and finally [formal] worship." Love did not mean for him a merely emotional feeling but, in his particular conditions, a conscious and intelligent effort to change the basic economic and social structures which produced the dire conditions in which people lived. Faith works itself out in love. And love must be efficacious. In today's world there is only one way to feed the hungry, clothe the naked, care for the sick and imprisoned—as Christ invited us to do: to change the structures of society which create and multiply every day those conditions. This is revolution. But his Cardinal Primate returned a formal response: "In the social realm, there are debatable issues, and the Church does not enter into debatable issues because its truth is permanent."

Camilo would not take this answer. He pressed his point: "Revolutionary action is a Christian, a priestly struggle." He was removed from his post at the university. When he made public his concrete option for social reform—a rather simple socialist program—the cardinal forbade him to speak further on social questions and denounced publicly his doctrines as "erroneous and pernicious." Camilo was "reduced to lay status" but he continued to consider himself a priest: "Revolutionary action is a priestly struggle." He was clear that political action was the key to change. His program was to gather and integrate all the groups interested in a revolutionary change in order to form a united front for elections. But the electoral possibility was a fraud. The pact between conservatives and liberals (both members of the same oppressing oligarchy) to take turns in government effectively ruled out the possibility of change in that direction. At the polls, the people had two choices—and both meant the same thing! Camilo preached abstention. But this was not enough. A general strike, peaceful disobedience was the next step. But this immediately unleashed repression. Thus, Torres was driven to admit that only a violent revolution could change things: "Now, the people do not believe in elections. The people know that legal means are at an end. . . . The people know that only armed rebellion is left. The people are desperate and ready to stake their lives so that the next generation of Colombians may not be slaves."[8] At this point, the Castroist movement offered the most efficient organization and Torres joined it. A dupe of communism? "I would rather be that than a dupe of the oligarchy." The name of Camilo belongs now to all revolutionaries in Latin America—Christians and non-Christians alike. A Marxist Uruguayan poet sings of the power of "Camilo's Cross" through which God himself calls from heaven for a revolution!

In 1952 a Brazilian priest was made bishop and assigned as auxiliary to the city of Rio. Born of a modest "secularist" couple of teachers at the beginning of the century, he had felt very early the vocation to the priesthood. As a passionate young man, he had militated in fascist and clerical movements of the right. In Rio, he had been concerned with the problems of education, gaining a new understanding of Brazilian society. In 1955, the famous Archbishop Gerlier of France suggested in a private conversation: "Why don't you place your ability at the service of the solution of the problem of the *favellas* (shanty towns)?" Dom Helder had more than once looked at the miserable huts and caves perched on the slopes around Rio. "I had felt the problem"—he reminisces—"but without getting involved in the struggle."[9] As he got involved, his views began to radicalize. The *favellas* yielded their secret; they were simply the open wounds of a sickness rooted in the bones and entrails of the country: exploitation, dependence, imperialism. He began to be vocal about it, and his denunciations touched the sore political, economic, social spots. "I am not an expert. . . . I am only a pastor who is there and sees his people suffer." His views estranged him more and more from the Archbishop of Rio. After the Vatican Council he was sent to the Northeast, the most submerged area in Brazil. He took possession of his diocese as the General Castello Branco led the triumphant coup which implanted a brutal right-wing dictatorship in Brazil with the support and under the leadership of the Pentagon and the State Department.

It is hardly necessary to dwell on the views and attitudes of the man who has become the living voice of the Christian conscience in Latin America, a little man whom the government and reactionaries slander and denounce but do not dare to touch: an aggressive and practical pacifist (armed revolt is today "legitimate but impossible in L.A.") who prefers to speak of "peaceful violence" and claims kinship with Martin Luther King; a passionate pastor who is night and day at the call of his people; an almost mystic who gets up every day at 2 A.M. to pray ("I really believe in Christ; for me Christ is not an abstraction; he is a personal friend"); a speaker who has denounced imperialism, oppression, tortures in crowded auditoriums in Chicago, Paris, or Tokyo; a fearless man whose secretary was killed and mutilated a year ago as a warning and who receives threatening phone calls throughout the night; a personal friend of the Pope and an outspoken critic of the Church ("the truth is that the Church still belongs to the power machine"). He follows the path that priestly love opens for him in today's Latin America. "The only judge I accept is God."

Archbishop Cámara has spoken openly on a number of things. Two of them deserve to be mentioned at this point. On the one hand, he has rejected any possibility of the Church remaining neutral:

> Let's get rid of the idea that the Church, after having committed so many atrocities, can now afford to sit back. It is our duty to offer leadership, yes, but without any pride, because we Christians are the most guilty.

For critics who extol the "spiritual" task of the Church he has a caustic answer: "I am trying to send men to heaven, not sheep. And certainly not sheep with their stomachs empty and their testicles crushed." This means a political option, which Dom Helder does not dodge: "I am a socialist." But he makes several things clear: "I think we can avail ourselves of the Marxist method of analysis, which is still valid, leaving aside the materialist conception of life." "But I don't see the solution in the socialist governments that exist today. . . . the Marxist record is awful." The basis of his socialism is both simple and far reaching: "God made man in his image and likeness, so he could become his co-creator and not a slave." "My socialism is a special one which respects the human person and turns to the gospel. My socialism is justice."

Men of the stature of Camilo Torres and Dom Helder Cámara are not legion. They are pioneers. But the number of lesser but equally committed Christians militating for liberation grows every day. It would be impossible to offer an adequate picture of this process.[10] A few notes will convey some impression of its extension and magnitude.

• Laymen who had militated in the social democratic parties and in Catholic Action movements related to them have radicalized their political views as they experienced the critical conditions, the failure of "development," and the retrenchment of their parties into alliances with the conservatives. Some move in the direction of armed struggle, others to student opposition, some to work for conscientization and politicization in slum areas and shanty towns, in trade unions and among peasants. The traditional Catholic lay organizations have as a consequence entered a severe crisis, and some new forms and groupings are taking their place (usually transconfessional and many times not exclusively Christian).

• Radicalization has moved much more rapidly among priests. In almost all countries groups of priests have organized to express and enact their denunciation and rejection of the existing system (economic, political, and social). Most of these groups have relations with revolutionary movements, and some have assumed a direct political participation. A number of collisions with the hierarchy has taken place, not around the common problems created in the affluent countries (celibacy, ordination) but concerning the role of the priest in the political and social life of the countries.

• The active participation of these groups is becoming a major fact in many countries. In Bolivia, for instance, Catholic and Protestant ministers and laymen gathered around ISAL (Church and Society in Latin America) were one of the important supports and incentives for change during the progressive government of General Juan José Torres. When the reactionary coup under Banzer took place in 1971, fifty Catholic and some ten Protestant ministers had to leave the country (a small Church like the Methodist lost three of its fifteen ministers to exile). Since then, no less than thirty priests and ministers have been put in jail. Nevertheless, only in December, 1972, one hundred priests published a manifesto entitled "Violence and the Gospel" denouncing repression, tortures, generalized governmental violence and the deteriorating situation for the people prevailing in Bolivia. In spite of the threat of the government, the Episcopal Conference found itself compelled to recognize the legitimacy and justice of the complaint.

• Unfortunately, it is more difficult to account for the Christian laymen participating in the struggle. A study conducted in Brazil by a congressman and journalist summarized the situation up to 1968, four years after the military coup took over government and unleashed the most organized, cruel, and relentless repression ever known in the continent. The persecution seems to have been particularly concerned with uprooting all efforts to develop among the people a critical consciousness, an awareness and a desire for political participation in society. Thus educational efforts among the people in the shanty towns, peasants' organizations, and student unions were the more thoroughly persecuted. The congressman Marcio Pereira Alves, after traveling thousands of miles throughout the country and investigating endless lists of persecuted, imprisoned, tortured, and accused people, reached the conclusion that "persecuted Christians represented one of the major groups victim of the military regime. And, as a group, they are the only ones who could be identified." This three-hundred-page book *The Christ of the People*[11] documents the systematic destruction of the MEB (Movement for Education at the Base), which used Paulo Freire's literacy and conscientization method to reach millions of people, of the Student Christian Union, and of many other paraecclesiastical organizations, as well as the story of many Christian laymen and ministers accused of subversion during that time. The situation has not changed since 1968.

• Foreign priests are a significant presence in a continent which has suffered from an endemic shortage of them since last century. Missionary priests come frequently from the "developed" world and often are committed to a progressive liberal view. Their radicalization is often even more rapid than that of local priests. Several Maryknoll missionaries became avowed supporters of guerrilla movements in Central America (the Melville brothers being the most conspicuous case). Dominicans, White Fathers, and Jesuits have been expelled from Brazil, Uruguay, and Paraguay as "subversive" (sometimes governments have exercised pressure on hierarchies and apostolic *nuncios* in order to obtain the removal of foreign missionary priests). A similar process takes place among some Protestant missionaries.

• A growing number of publications articulate the viewpoints and reflection of these Christians. Frequently, they are precarious, often mimeographed, publications. Some are short-lived by reason of governmental or ecclesiastical censorship, lack of means, or simply excess of work. Some, nevertheless, have become significant means of expression for the whole continent. *Cristianismo y sociedad,* published by ISAL, *Víspera,* a Catholic independent monthly published in Montevideo, *Enlace,* the publication of the Argentine Priests for the Third World, CIDOC (Center for Intercultural Documentation in Cuernavaca, Mexico) are only the best known. Two significant collections of pronouncements by priests and Catholic groups have appeared in the last five years: *Iglesia Latinoamericana, ¿protesta o profecía?* edited by Rossi (Buenos, Aires: Editorial Galerna, 1970), and *L'Eglise rebelle de l'Amérique Latine* edited by Gheerbardt (Paris: Editions du Seuil, 1970).

The brief mention of groups of priests made above demands some amplification. Three samples will give a sense of the unity and variety of these organizations.

In Argentina, the "Priests for the Third World" were born of a meeting of two bishops and some priests in Quilmes in 1965. In the light of Vatican II, they were asking questions such as "Who is God for us?", "Who are we in the world?", "What is the Church for?" The simple response stresses "the solidarity of the priest with his people in their concrete situation." In the ensuing years there were multiple opportunities for the expression of this solidarity—local labor conflicts, police repression, violence done to slum dwellers and squatter populations, the "Christian" claim of the fascist military government of General Onganía. In almost all cases the bishops rebuked or punished their actions.

When eighteen bishops from different areas of the third world (Africa, Asia, Latin America) issued a manifesto in 1967,[12] some of the priests involved in this conflict invited a national meeting to consider their responsibility. Surprisingly enough, more than one hundred priests turned up. Since then, the movement has grown to more than five hundred—practically the whole younger priesthood in the country. Challenged by the hierarchy as to their theological and spiritual basis, they produced one of the most cogent and balanced documents, a pronouncement showing the maturity and depth of their Christian concern and their social commitment. A few sentences from a discussion of prophecy and politics deserve mention:

> Our age is experiencing a return to prophecy. . . . What especially irritates and disconcerts some people is that this transformation of the Church implies with ever greater clarity a political engagement. . . . Political engagement implies certain concrete and debat-

able options; it demands analysis, strategy, tactics . . . do these belong to the universe of faith? Can they be justified by recourse to the prophets? . . . Comparison of certain traits of prophecy with contemporary events has convinced us that neither can there be true prophetic denunciation nor true prophetic promise unless prophecy be.applied to politics, unless it discerns among political options those which are more in accord with its interpretation of reality. . . . Thus, for example, themes developed by prophecy are justice, freedom, the future of man. . . . Prophecy emerges . . . in crises, when one world is dying and another is being born. . . . Prophecy scrutinizes the signs of the times. . . . These signs are today "the rebellion of youth," "the struggle for freedom," "the search for and formulation of a socialism with a human countenance." At the same time, prophecy and politics are two distinct realities and their autonomy must be preserved.[13]

Since that declaration, two important decisions should be recorded. In the first place, the organization has indicated its option for Peronism, defining it as a critical option, not for a particular party but for a movement in which the people (particularly the lower classes) have found an identity and the possibility of becoming active participants in the shaping of their own future. Secondly, they have articulated their support of a socialism which will be national (responding "to the uniqueness of our people"), popular (enabling the people to participate and decide), Latin American, humanistic (giving place to the spiritual, cultural, and ethical fullfillment of man), and critical (allowing for a constant renewal).

Argentina is one of the most modern countries in Latin America. Peru, on the other hand, has one of the longest and most classical histories. The conquerors found there one of the three most developed Indian cultures: the Incas. They took possession of the country swiftly, implanted one of their basic headquarters on the continent, divided the land, subjected the Indians to practical slavery, and exploited their rich mines. It became one of the most developed centers for the Church. The Peruvian colonial Church councils legislated the organization of the Church and the fight against heresy, magic, and paganism. Its capital was the seat of the Inquisition. But the religion of the Indians in the highlands *(sierras)* was the formal Catholicism mixed with the cult of the Pachamama (the Indian goddess Earth). The aristocratic control of the country has lasted in Peru up to the present, in spite of populist movements in the twenties. The alliance of the Church with the aristocracy characterized Peru.

Suddenly, a military coup took over power in 1968. Against all precedents it announced nationalization of foreign interests, and agrarian reform and several other socialist-oriented laws. The U.S.A. threatened with the Hickenlooper amendment. The local oligarchy, supported by the "liberal" press it owns, erected its defenses. But three months before, a group of sixty priests had issued a declaration which the Cardinal Primate publicly supported. Backed by telling statistics, they described the tragic situation of the people. They diagnosed the causes: "the unjust distribution of capital and land property" (there was a careful discussion of the rural situation), "the surrender of the national patrimony to the large imperialist monopolies," "a defective juridico-institutional structure," and "an inadequate cultivation of responsibility." The ground root of these evils was the capitalist system of production and ownership. This was the first obstacle, which had to be overcome in order to make possible other reforms.

Twenty-eight other priests joined the original sixty. The movement, known as ONIS, defined more concretely their views and action. Some two hundred and fifty priests (two out of every seven) adhered to it; four bishops have also joined. Contrary to the Argentinian case, the hierarchy has backed it. Most of the priests belonging to ONIS work in the slums around Lima, some among students, a few in the country. In 1969 three hundred priests wrote to the episcopate: they requested a greater speed both in terms of the renewal of the Church (separate the Church from the state, thus giving greater freedom to both; "simplify 'the face of the Church'": dresses,

52

protocol, titles, and dignities), and of the social transformations (denounce existing injustices, support the workers in their demands). ONIS is thus acting as a stimulus, inciting the government to move faster and more radically, trying to prevent the middle way chosen from ending into a merely modernized capitalism. There is little theological elaboration in the documents published so far. They simply trace back their positions to the social doctrine of the Church as defined in Vatican II and the latest encyclicals (mainly *Populorum Progressio*). On the other hand, one of them, Gustavo Gutiérrez, has written a most explicit exposition of the theology of liberation which will occupy us later.[14]

Colombia, the land of Camilo Torres, is the place in Latin America where both law and history give the Church the greatest power in the social and political life. When a group of sixty priests in Golconda drew an analysis of the situation quite similar to that of ONIS in Peru, the response of the hierarchy was altogether different. Some of the signatories were suspended. The priests accused the army of genocide against the Indians in Guahiba. Four priests were accused of subversion and put in prison for calling the approaching election "a farce." The Archbishop (a man of aristocratic tradition) repeatedly rejected the positions of the priests.

It is interesting to summarize some aspects of the Golconda Pronouncement[15] inasmuch as it offers some new elements. The first one is an insistence on the fact that "good will is not enough: we need to know objective reality as it is" and, later on, we have "the need to elaborate a scientific methodology of investigation and work" in order to avoid empiricism or a fruitless activism. At this point, it anticipates some of the Santiago emphases mentioned in the previous chapter. On the other hand, there is an effort to support the stand of a solid theological argument: (1) the inclusion of "'the temporal' in God's purpose and plan of salvation," breaking the dichotomy between the temporal and the eternal ("without falling into

53

confusion, we must constantly stress the deep unity between God's saving purpose fulfilled in Jesus Christ and human aspirations, between the history of salvation and human history . . . excluding all dichotomies"); (2) consequently faith cannot be understood as mere intellectual assent to doctrine but as "an attitude of engagement, in the light of God's design, with everything human, whether individual, social, economic, political, educational. . . ." (3) Finally, the analysis and understanding of faith result in a program of action aiming at "cooperating in the political education of the citizens," "the support and stimulation of people's efforts to create and develop their own organizations," and "a task of 'conscientization' and social education." The document then develops these tasks in terms of social, economic, and political goals and liturgical, catechetical, and evangelistic ministries, including serious demands for the internal reformation of the Church and the elimination of its ties with the oppressive system.

Foregoing the presentation of similar groups existing in most of the other Latin American countries, we shall move, before closing this chapter, to a Protestant-initiated organization: "Church and Society in Latin America," usually known as ISAL. Partly imported as an extension of the ecumenical interest in the problem of development, ISAL was born in a conference in Huampani (Peru) attended by people from Protestant churches concerned with social problems.[16] Successive meetings in 1966, 1967, and 1971 marked the rapid transformation of ISAL's conception of itself, its relation to the churches, and its role in Latin America. In the first few years (1960–65) the analysis of the situation, which at the beginning oscillated between a developmentalist and a revolutionary approach, gained greater consistency, adopted the "sociology of dependence" (structured around the notion of neocolonialism and dependence) and made a clear revolutionary and socialist option. This ideological clarification was followed in the years 1966–68 by a transformation in the theological perspective,

54

veering from a predominantly Barthian theology to a "theology of God's transforming action in history" greatly indebted to Paul Lehmann and Richard Shaull until Rubem Alves gave it a creative expression in critical dialogue with Marcuse on the one hand and Moltmann on the other. At the same time, ISAL became more critical of its relation with the churches. The churches could not follow the theological and ideological definition of ISAL and the latter criticized the isolation in which the Protestant churches had lived as "cultural enclaves" more closely related to the overseas metropolis than to their own environment. The option for a Marxist analysis and interpretation had now been consciously adopted. But it was not a mere stereotype, and interpretations varied from a "Cuban-type" socialism to a Marcusian "esoteric" Marxism.

Since that time ISAL has been in search of greater political engagement. Both for reason of its Protestant origin and its intellectual constituency, it lived in a somewhat artificial ideological tower. Since 1970, it has more and more defined its own function as "mobilization of the people." This, in turn, has brought it back to a greater interest in the churches and an emphasis on local (national) movements rather than centralized action. National ISAL groups tend to become more independent.

> Our concern is not so much to characterize "dependence" and to define the groups which make for its continuation, but to ask, *How can it be overcome?* The victory over dependence will not result from a miracle or from the inexorable and magic fulfillment of a historical process. In order to achieve it we must impel the organization of those sectors of the people who are exploited by national dominant classes and by imperialism.[17]

This clear ideological and strategical definition demands a theology which does not attempt a systematic, overall explanation (and consequently there is great mistrust of imported theologies) but understands itself as Christian reflection born of daily active engagement.

Repeated allusions to the conflicts between the pioneering revolutionary groups of Christians and their ecclesiastical hierarchies could lead to the wrong impression that the latter are uniformly and blindly entrenched in reactionary positions. The situation changes from country to country and from church to church. The association with the traditional oligarchies and with their liberal capitalist successors is deeply rooted and lasting and, in some cases, strong enough to enlist local bishops or national (Catholic or Protestant) hierarchies as wholehearted supporters. Groups of prominent laymen, organized as defenders of "tradition, family, and property" or "religion, country, and home" agitate the ghost of communism and coerce or cajole the hierarchies into supporting some of their positions. Organized religious movements of fascist tendency, such as the "Cursillismo," the "Knights of Columbus" or "Opus Dei," reach in some cases significant victories (notably they ascended to government in Argentina with General Onganía in 1966-69). But, on the whole, the situation is far more complex and nuanced.

The impact of revolutionary forces among the ministry of the churches and the evidence of the conditions they describe and denounce is far too strong to be ignored. With a varying mixture of decision, enthusiasm, reluctance, and uncertainty, the official pronouncements of the churches are nevertheless forced to reflect the new prophetic temper. Once the conflicting arena of history is exposed at world level, no Church can isolate religion from what is happening around it. And this leads in Latin America inevitably to a denunciation of the existing order. Ecclesiastical pronouncements vary in the depth, motivation, and force of their analysis and commitment. Some limit themselves to deplore the existing evils and to exhort the rich and the powerful to grant a larger measure of justice and welfare. Now, more and more move to a more structural analysis of the situation and request basic transformations of the organization of society. At this point perhaps the clearest and most significant example has been the Second General Meeting of the Latin American Conference of Bishops (of the Roman Catholic Church) which took place in Medellín in 1968.[18] Although the documents from that meeting are not altogether coherent, they are all permeated by a recognition of dependence and structural injustice as the root problem. A total *transformation* is called for (the loaded words *development* and *revolution* are avoided) and the Church pledges itself to participate in this change through its educational, "conscientizing," and inspirational ministry. At a much more modest scale, the Bolivian and Argentine pronouncements of the Methodist Church can also be mentioned, in which they expressly reject the capitalist system and urge the Methodist people to participate actively in the shaping of a new and more human society.[19] Local pronouncements by bishops and synods go sometimes much further. Notably, a number of bishops in Puerto Rico, Brazil, Mexico, Peru, and several other places have openly avowed their support of a socialist system.

The chasm between these progressive and even revolutionary pronouncements and the thought and action of the revolutionary groups we have presented is, nevertheless, much wider than what the written statements tend to suggest. It is caused, it seems to me, at two interrelated points. One is the reluctance of Church authorities to admit an ideological option, particularly one related to Marxism. Their view of the situation tends, therefore, to become descriptive; their analyses lack unity and accuracy, and their proposals are vague. Back of this is the fear of breaking the unity of the Church: a Church which understands itself as the Church of both the conservative and the progressive, the reactionary and the revolutionary, of the right and of the left cannot commit itself ideologically. The other point is the fear of calling the oppressed and exploited to work out their own liberation. This is due to two reasons: the fact that the hierarchies are more closely linked with the dominant classes and tend to address their exhortations to them, and the fear to incite a class struggle which may lead to violence. But these two points are precisely the decisive ones for a revolutionary consciousness. Unless the qualitative jump is taken, we are still moving within the realm of reformism and liberalism. There are deep theological as well as practical issues involved in this distinction, which we shall try to explore in the following chapters.

NOTES

[1] Concerning the idea of "historical project" see the discussion of Gera's theological view in Chapter Four below and the remarks of Hugo Assmann in *Opresión-Liberación: Desafío a los cristianos* (Montevideo: Tierra Nueva, 1971), pp. 169-173.

[2] The cultural aspect has been particularly emphasized by Darcy Ribeiro, in *Las Américas y la Civilización* (Buenos Aires: Siglo Veintiuno, 1970). More important even is the emphasis on the awakening of a critical consciousness which informs all the work of the Brazilian educationist Paulo Freire. See n. 11 below and the anthology *Conciencia y Revolución* (Montevideo: Tierra Nueva, 1969).

[3] Cf. the much quoted "letter" of Guevara to the left-wing Uruguayan journal *Marcha*, "El Socialismo y el Hombre en Cuba," *Obras Completas* (Buenos Aires: Ediciones del Plata, 1967), vol. II, pp. 7-27.

[4] "Documento Final," part I, 2.6 and Introducción.

[5] "Evangelio y Praxis de Liberación," in *Misión Abierta*, nos. 8-9 (Madrid, September/October, 1972), pp. 455-456. It is the opening statement of Gutiérrez's presentation at the "Escorial meeting," published together with the other contributions to that meeting in Borrat, Comblin, Dussel, et al., *Fe Cristiana y Cambio Social en América Latina.*

[6] *Habla Fidel Castro sobre los cristianos revolucionarios,* ed. Hugo Assmann (Montevideo: Tierra Nueva, 1972), pp. 40, 46. The setting of these declarations of Castro, which Assmann discusses in his introduction, is very significant, and rules out a mere tactical interpretation.

[7] There are numerous publications in English of Camilo Torres's writings. The best two are edited by John Gerassi, *Camilo Torres, Revolutionary Priest, The Complete Writings & Messages of Camilo Torres* (New York: Random House, Vintage, 1971), and by Maurice Zeitlin, *Father Camilo Torres, Revolutionary Writings* (New York: Harper & Row, 1972).

[8] "Message to Colombians from the Mountains," *Camilo Torres, Revolutionary Priest,* p. 423. The quotations used here come from his

messages and letters. But these more dramatic appeals should not be read in isolation from the analytical, sociological, and theological writings of Camilo.

⁹ The quotations used here are taken from an interview published in *Siete Días Ilustrados* (Buenos Aires, October 5, 1970). It has been published in English by LADOC (Documentation Service of the Latin American Bureau, U.S. Catholic Conference, Washington, D.C.), no. 19 (June, 1971). The best source in English for Dom Helder Cámara is the translation of José de Broucker's book *Dom Helder Cámara; the Violence of a Peacemaker* (Maryknoll, N.Y.: Orbis Books, 1970).

¹⁰ Among the many reports concerning Christians committed to the struggle for liberation in Latin America, we recommend the excellent summary and bibliography in Dussel, *Historia,* pp. 168-277. A more concise presentation can be found in Gutiérrez, *A Theology of Liberation,* pp. 101-131. The INDAL documentation center (220 Waversebaan, 3030 Haverlee, Belgium) has published a series of excellent dossiers, of which particularly no. 8, *La Iglesia ante los problemas socio-políticos,* is very relevant.

¹¹ Marcio Moreira Alves, *O Cristo do Povo* (Rio de Janeiro: Sabia, 1968). An excellent account of the Movement for Education at the Base (MEB), Freire's project, and other aspects of the struggle of Christians in Brazil is given by Emanuel de Kadt, *Catholic Radicals in Brazil* (London: Oxford University Press, 1970). Two other publications deserve mention: a dossier published by ISAL, *La Iglesia cuestiona el milagro brasileño* (Santiago de Chile: Secretaría de Estudios, 1973), and the article "Catholic Church turns back on generals" in the *Brazilian Information Bulletin* (Berkeley, Calif.: American Friends of Brazil, Box 2279, Station A, Berkeley, Calif. 94702), no. 10 (June, 1973).

¹² "A Letter to the Peoples of the Third World," *Between Honesty and Hope,* pp. 3-12.

¹³ *Sacerdotes para el Tercer Mundo* (Buenos Aires; Oficina de Publicaciones del Movimiento, 1970). The main theological document, "Argentina: Priests for the Third World," has been published in English by IDOC-NA (IDOC-NA, Inc., 637 W. 125 Street, New York, N.Y. 10027), no. 15 (December 12, 1970), pp. 58-96.

¹⁴ *Between Honesty and Hope,* pp. 74 ff. reproduces the 1968 document and several pastoral letters on the social situation. An excellent report on the Church in Peru has appeared in the Argentine pastoral journal, *Actualidad Pastoral,* no. 54 (Buenos Aires: Editorial Bonum).

¹⁵ *Between Honesty and Hope,* pp. 85-93.

¹⁶ Reports of the several ISAL conferences and the ISAL publications can be requested from the central office (ISAL, Uruguay 1255, Montevideo, Uruguay). The proceedings of the Santiago de Chile

Conference of 1966 have been published in English by Jorge Lara-Braud, *Social Justice and the Latin Churches* (Richmond: John Knox Press, 1969). It includes a valuable analysis of the development in the thinking of ISAL during the first decisive years (pp. 9-19).

[17] *América Latina: movilización popular y fe cristiana* (Report of the Ñaña Conference of 1971, Montevideo, ISAL, 1971), p. 143.

[18] See above, n. 8 in Chapter Two.

[19] "Manifiesto al pueblo de Bolivia," statement of the Bolivian Methodist Church at the proclamation of its autonomy, March, 1970. James Goff has published an English translation. See also his article, "Setback in Bolivia," *Christianity and Crisis,* vol. 32, no. 5 (New York, April 3, 1972), pp. 83-84. The "Statement on the National Situation" of the Methodist Church in Argentina can be obtained from the office of the Church (Belgrano 3876, Buenos Aires, Argentina).

Chapter Four

The Theology
of Liberation

It may seem strange to devote half of a book supposedly dealing with theology to a discussion of sociological analysis and political trends and options, only to arrive belatedly to the consideration of the theology that undergirds the positions taken by Christians. To have followed an inverse procedure would, nevertheless, have been misleading with regard to this theology. It would have suggested that somehow a theology of liberation (or "for" liberation, or "in the context of the struggle for liberation," as I would prefer to say) was first developed and then people began to follow the course of action appropriate to it. Latin American theology of liberation is beginning to emerge (as all theology?) *after the fact,* as the reflection about facts and experiences which have already evoked a response from Christians. This response, undertaken as Christian obedience, is not the mere result of theological deduction, or of political theory. It is a total, synthetic act, many times going far beyond what one can at the moment justify theologically. Then, as one is called to explain, to understand the full meaning or to invite other Christians to follow the same path, a theology is slowly born.

Such theology, nevertheless, has not developed in isolation. It builds on the biblical and theological renewal in Europe and the U.S.A., both in the Roman and in the Protestant churches. The new names we shall be discussing—Rubem Alves, Gustavo Gutiérrez, Julio de Santa Ana, Juan Luis Segundo, Hugo

Assmann, or more dramatically Camilo Torres or Helder Camara—belong to men steeped in the theological tradition of Europe or the U.S.A. and in constant dialogue with it. Protestant Barthian and post-Barthian theology, Roman Catholic conciliar and post-conciliar thought, with their common emphasis on the dynamism of God's action, the historical character of the Christian faith, the concreteness of incarnation, the future-oriented nature of an eschatological faith—all of this has had a very significant influence. Nevertheless, this budding Latin American theology is not a mere reproduction, adaptation, or transcription of the "academic theology" of the traditional centers. These theologians are increasingly claiming their right to "mis-read" their teachers, to find their own insertion in the theological tradition, to offer their own interpretation of the theological task.

In order to present this theology, which we shall discuss critically later on, we shall attempt three things. Firstly, and more extensively, we shall look at four of the most significant theologians. Secondly, we shall try to suggest a comparative interpretation of this theology in relation to current European and American theologies. Thirdly, we shall conclude that the theologians with whom we are dealing are raising, not merely a new theological subject, but a new way of doing theology, which in turn poses some important problems. This new way and these problems open the possibility for a fruitful—though conflictive—dialogue between Northern- and Southern-based theology.[1]

Juan Luís Segundo,[2] an Uruguayan Jesuit, is perhaps the most "ecumenical" of the young Latin American Catholic theologians in terms of his deep roots in European theology, his interest in tradition, and the range of his theological interests. It is not easy to summarize Segundo's thought, which develops itself in rich and suggestive analyses. It is possible to characterize his theology, using the title of one of his works, as "an open theology for adult laymen." He starts from Karl Rahner's anthropology, which attempts to overcome the dichotomy of nature and grace by conceiving man (humanity) in his very creaturehood as open to God. Faith, therefore, humanizes man, fulfills him as man, leads him to the realization of his proper destiny. There is no split between faith and man's growth in humanity and therefore between the Church—the community of those who "know" the meaning of humanity—and humanity, which is a Church "latent." Segundo assumes this vision and translates it to the ethical and social realms. He does the former through the notion of love. This is, in fact, the concrete meaning of man's openness to the divine; this is the meaning of human existence which the Church knows, announces, and exemplifies and toward which mankind moves. The gospel could thus be translated in the formula "no love is lost in this world." The Church, consequently, exists for the sake of mankind, as a sign of the meaning of God's purpose which is at the same time man's fulfillment.

In the sociopolitical area, this implies a discernment of the direction of history, of "the signs of the times." Segundo's philosophy of history is in this respect deeply influenced by Teilhard de Chardin, inasmuch as it regards history as a movement of the universe itself toward ever richer and more complex syntheses of existence, culminating in a point which coincides with the Christian eschatological vision. As far as the interpretation of the present time is concerned, his thought follows, as I see it, a dialectic combining three criteria. One is the analysis of society: its problems and possible solutions, the balance of alternatives or possibilities. Therefore, he insists that his thought moves "from society to theology." The second criterion is "a sense of what is right" which a collective consciousness possesses, a sense of "the direction in which things are moving" which man—certainly not individually and in isolation but collectively and in solidarity—cannot but discern (we must at this point recall the anthropological basis). Thirdly, there is the text of Scripture and the tradition, interpreted in the situation and in the line of God's universal purpose of redemption. Concretely applied, this dialectic points in a twofold way in the same direction: on the one hand, toward a greater human maturity, to the man come-of-age who takes responsibility for his existence and the history of humanity (not individually but in solidary love); on the other hand, toward a socialization, which is precisely the collective and free fulfillment of this human plenitude. (Segundo is, of course, aware of the distance between this direction and any sociopolitical form which man can create along this path).

This history-saving direction gives Segundo the possibility of a penetrating and creative critique of both the theological tradition and present ecclesiastical practice. He can thus perceive, for instance, the liberating power inherent in the early Trinitarian and christological formulae. He can also criticize sacramental or religious conceptions which attempt to protect man from the risks and responsibilities of history, instead of being signs of the sacrificial engagement of redemptive love. Segundo's thought becomes thus very concrete, both in the reinterpretation of doctrine and in the renewal of ecclesiastical practice. In the latter aspect, at variance with other men we shall see, he has a great interest in the "inner life" of the Church and propounds an alternative to the traditional pastoral practice of his Church. This practice is directed to the masses, based in the religious immaturity of the people, and exercised through the institutions of a society closely linked with the Church. Such means are less and less available in an increasingly secularized consumer society; on the other hand, they do not correspond to the nature of the gospel and the Church. Instead of them, Segundo suggests a minority Church, which is composed of communities of historical engagement and a sacramental practice related to it; a Church which will be a true sign of redemption and of man's destiny. He has frequently been criticized as an "elitist." In response, he has clarified the relation between the elite and the mass or, as he would rather put it, between "massive" and "reflected" behaviors, a distinction which corresponds analogically to that between humanity and the Church and which cuts through the behavior of every community and every Christian individual. Reflected or elitist actions are destined to serve the mass; the latter, on the other hand, cannot as such concentrate the energy necessary to move toward higher and more human levels unless their path is opened by elitist actions.

In contrast with this thought, we find the approach of the advocates of a "popular pastoral practice," assuming "folk-Catholicism" and developing the values implicit in it. Interestingly enough, this distinction corresponds also to different political conceptions and different revolutionary strategies. We shall call attention to one of the most lucid exponents of "a theology of the people," Lucio Gera, an Argentine priest, theological adviser to the "Priests for the Third World," and a member of the Vatican's Pontifical Theological Committee.[3]

Gera begins with the simple question: What is the Church for? What is its mission? Interpreting classical doctrine, in accord with the Council's definitions, he answers: "The mission of the Church is to implant faith in the world through the proclamation of the gospel and to promote man in the realm of temporal values" (I/2). These are not to be understood as two independent, merely juxtaposed or outwardly connected tasks but as innerly connected, mutually interpenetrating dimensions of one single mission. In one sense, all of Gera's theology makes this unity explicit, avoiding at the same time all forms of reductionism or loss of identity of each one of the dimensions.

The unity is perceived in two complementary ways. On the one hand, each term is "ordered" or "destined" to the other by the very nature of the gospel, which is directed to the same man and seeks his total and unified realization. Therefore "as [it] fulfills the task of implanting faith [the Church] promotes temporal values," and, as it does the latter, it does it "in view of the faith" (I/3). On the other hand, the mission of the Church is not

65

exercised in a vacuum but in history (in a culture, among a people) and in relation to a particular historical project.

The central nucleus of evangelization—the task of the Church—is the *kerygma* (which can be enunciated theologically: "God is the one Father of all men and peoples"; christologically: "Christ, sent by the Father, has died and risen for our salvation"; soteriologically: "man must be converted and stop sinning"). The proclamation of the kerygma elicits faith, "a typical relation of man with God, with Christ." This situation, "experienced as something transcendent on the spiritual and religious level," means a liberation from sin which must be made explicit "in the concrete life of man" (IV/13-14). A first form of explication takes place in the realm of values, because this liberation, as relation to God, "immediately contains and determines other values of relation": to the neighbor, whose absolute dignity it recognizes (fraternity versus domination as the form of relationship) and to nature, conceived as subordinated to man (and consequently the primacy of the political over the economic, of the relation to man over that to nature).

This first example remains still at a level of abstraction (which is not equivalent for Gera to "unreal" but rather to "germinal"). Evangelization itself, nevertheless, demands a further step; one that carries the Church beyond this abstract level: the translation of these values in terms of outward forms of organization, institutions, structures, forms of conduct. This second level is determined by the fact that the kerygma is not addressed to mere individuals but to a people, "to a collective subject, a society" (IV/5). Faith seeks rootage in a collective historical subject "and not simply in the sum total of individuals." These collective subjects are peoples with their culture, their particular ways, their organic consciousness. These are the conditions in which the kerygma and its values will become concrete. In such a process two facts must be considered. One, having to do with the kerygma itself, concerns its eschatological transcendence: the fullness of salvation "comes at the end and not within time" (III/2). Consequently, evangelization de-nounces every utopia, every claim "of reaching man's goal in an immanent eschatology," every affirmation "that history might by itself lead to an earthly paradise." The other fact, having to do with the collective subject to whom the gospel is addressed, underlines the importance of understanding that peoples realize themselves in history, projecting their future and concentrating in that project all their strength and abilities. Consequently "the mission of the Church as a promoter of temporal values does not consist only ... in announcing great principles or values but in giving to them a concrete expression ... paying attention *to the historical project* which is under way" (I/9). For this purpose, the Church must be able to discern this historical project and to relate to it the kerygmatic values it proclaims: this is the prophetic function of the Church, which can only be properly performed when it lives close to the peo-ple, identifying itself with them in such a way that it may be able to grasp their aspirations and to interpret them in relation to those values.

Gera does not ignore the hermeneutical problems involved in these affirmations or the sociological debate around the notion of people and historical project. We shall have occasion to return to some of these questions. Before closing this section, however, we find it more profitable to point out briefly the concrete form that these programmatic lines take in his thought. In order to move from the formal to the material, Gera describes the Latin American situation, which he sees as "a becoming aware of the historical situation of dependence" (IV/6). The form of consciousness corresponding to this aware-ness is "a project of liberation." The Latin American people "becomes today intimately aware of their domination and in-timately *decides* their LIBERATION." Dependence and liberation are not abstract enunciations: they mean cultural liberation (breaking away from the liberal-Enlightenment-magisterial culture in order to cultivate a culture of the people), political liberation (from the power of "the empire" which is at present represented by the U.S.A. and its local oligarchic clientele), and structural liberation (the end of the bourgeois state and the creation of a different shape of society, a socialist one).

We are now able to arrive, finally, to some definite proposals: (1) There is a definite, particular option involved for the Church. It has to *decide* in favor of a given system at a given time and to support it (III/7). Therefore, the Church participates in politics. It may make the wrong choice, to be sure, but it cannot avoid making one. In this light one must understand the option of the Priests of the Third World for Peronism in Argentina. (2) This political action of the Church stops, however, this side of access to political power. The mission of the Church is a prophetic one, and its power is therefore the power of the *word* (it announces, denounces, exhorts, teaches, but "it has not been given the task of exercising political power") (III/7). (3) A historical project is always an open-ended task: the Church participates in a people's project both assuming its aspirations and pushing them critically toward a fuller realization. (4) This latter function requires that the Church will understand and accept the values implicit in the people itself. There is here a place for the appreciation of values implicit in folk-Catholicism but, even more significantly, in the very life of the people. The most important concrete value in the life of the people (it is the "poor people," the "marginals" which are here mainly in question) is solidarity, the will to be a community. (5) But this value of solidarity must be permeated with the kerygmatic value of justice, joining both in such a way that the people's consciousness of its destiny may be at the same time consolidated and deepened. This is the concrete situation in which the Church is called to support a "socialist" project, not as something already done, as a ready-made system, but as something which is "created along the way" (IV/7). The Church does not offer a model which it has itself invented; it does not impose a system from above (as in colonial Christianity), but it accompanies the people, "communicating the liberating contents derived from the kerygma." This is "a liberating evangelization."

The "theology of the people" breathes a certain trust in the "popular consciousness"—perhaps a secularized form of the traditional Roman Catholic doctrine of the *sensus fidelium* as a theological criterium. On the other hand, and correspondingly, there is an emphasis on the national character of the socialism it propounds and a mistrust of foreign ideologies, particularly of Marxism (without ignoring, to be sure, its analytical significance). In contrast to this, we must sketch the work of some theologians, characterized by a greater critical and ideological rigor. They are, properly speaking, the creators of "a theology of liberation." Among the many names which could be mentioned in this respect, we shall refer to the Peruvian priest Gustavo Gutiérrez and the Brazilian Hugo Assmann.

This theology is closely related to the development of sociological thought in Latin America. When sociology assumes the problem of dependence and liberation as a basic structure of analysis, displaces the liberal meaning of "liberty" with the revolutionary meaning of "liberation," and rearranges its categories and tools according to this new perspective, theology discovers a new direction for its own reflection. To be sure, it is not a merely theoretical discovery; rather the new sociological categories provided the scientific structure necessary to grasp, analyze, and carry forward a phenomenon for which the theologian had no categories: the revolutionary praxis of a growing number of Christians. Gutiérrez insists that this praxis is the point of departure of a theology of liberation. This does not attempt to buttress or justify such practice but to deepen it and give an account of it. In doing it, it finds that the ground has been explored by sociologists and it avails itself of their work.

Gutiérrez[4] is the man who has more carefully traced both the continuity between traditional theological thought on sociopolitical matters and this new perspective and the discontinuity between them. The very notion of liberation, for instance, has a long theological tradition, but has gained recently a breadth of meaning which is new. The value of a term such as this is that it makes it possible to understand the aspirations of peoples and social classes, to conceive history as a process and to speak of man's relation to God as one and the same reality, although differentiated in three levels of meaning: sociopolitical liberation, humanization as a historical process of man's self-realization, and deliverance from sin (fellowship between man and man and man and God). The originality of this theology is not to have discovered these three levels of meaning but to have started from their *unity* as the fundamental point of departure. It seems to me, in fact, that the clue to this theology is "the elimination of all and every dualism" (p. 60). This is why it criticizes and rejects "the distinction of realms" which characterized the last phase of the "social doctrine" of the Catholic Church. Gutiérrez underlines this unity by referring to "the one vocation to salvation" of all humanity (in terms similar to those we met in Segundo). Thus "the action of man in history, whether Christian or non-Christian gains . . . religious significance" (p. 72). The three levels constitute, therefore, a unity assumed by the Christian by virtue of his faith in "the recapitulation of all things in Christ." Sociopolitical struggle, human maturity, reconciliation with God, do not belong to different realms but to a single saving reality. God's grace and man's task are therefore also united. The same basic premise is also expressed in the affirmation that there is "only one history," (pp. 153ff.) inaugurated in Creation as the beginning both of "the human enterprise and of Yahweh's saving history" (p. 154). The exodus points to the unity between the sociopolitical and the redemptive dimensions, and this liberation is fulfilled and deepened in Jesus Christ. Every promise has a historical *locus* which points beyond itself, both historically and eschatologically. There are not two histories: one sacred and one profane or secular. The one history in which God acts is the history of men; it is in this history where we find God. There is only one "Christ-fulfilled" history (p. 153). All the chapters in Gutiérrez's presentation take this fundamental unity to different areas of theological thought. The couples liberation/salvation, love of the neighbor/Christology, politics/eschatology, humanity/Church, human solidarity/sacraments, cover the classical *loci* of theology indissolubly relating them to the search for sociopolitical liberation and the building of a new humanity.

We have already indicated that the thought of these men is characterized by a strict scientific-ideological analysis, avowedly Marxist. This is clearly seen in their way of relating praxis and theory and in their insistence on the rationality, conflict, and radicality of the political realm. It can also be seen in the recognition of class struggle. This assumption of Marxism—which is not tantamount to an uncritical acceptance of all its philosophy—is decisive for the theological task and indicates, as Giulio Girardi has said, "a qualitative leap" from the humanist or spiritualist inspiration of the "social concern" to an engagement mediated through a scientific (Marxist) analysis. How is this relation established? It is quite evident that one cannot expect to extract from the Bible models of political or economic organization applicable to society. Gutiérrez solves the problem by distinguishing two levels: that of political action, which is eminently rational/scientific and that of faith which is the liberation from sin and the access to fellowship with God and with all men. But there is also, he adds, a third, intermediate level: *utopia,* in which man projects his quest for a new man in a new society. The utopia stimulates science by putting forward a project which goes beyond the present horizon and demands the creation of new instruments and new hypotheses. Faith, in its turn, inspired by the vision of the final liberation, stirs utopian imagination to the creation of these proleptic and propelling visions. "Faith and political action do not relate to each other except through the project of creation of a new type of man in a different society, through utopia . . ." (p. 236).

Critics have not taken long in objecting to the fact that this theology, with its insistence on praxis and the sociopolitical context as privileged theological *data*, gives to the historical circumstances a determinative weight in theology. This is, according to Assmann,[5] precisely the significance of this theology. The idealism of the "rich world" believes that it can start from abstract conceptions and objective sources. It deceives itself: it only succeeds in idealizing the existing situation and projecting it afterward—thus the "theology of the death of God" and the "theology of secularization" project the conditions of the technological world. The only possible point of departure is the concrete situation. It is therefore very urgent to unmask the ideologies hidden in the theologies of the past (as we saw in Segundo) and to assume the historical character of theological reflection. We do theology "beginning from concreteness," from "particular realities."

This is the reason why we begin from a praxis. It is not merely that theology is at the service of action, as in a way it was in the old Jesuit order: seeing, judging, acting. Rather action is itself the truth. Truth is at the level of history, not in the realm of ideas. Reflection on praxis, on human significant action, can only be authentic when it is done from within, in the vicinity of the strategic and tactical plane of human action. Without this, reflection would not be critical and projective conscience; it would not be a revision and projection of praxis as such (p. 90). Another point mentioned in a different connection also belongs here: a praxis is not simply subjective or arbitrary; it means that a situation has been analyzed and assumed by means of an interpretative synthesis. In this way, the sociopolitical analysis and the ideological option implicit in it, which are included in the praxis adopted, are determinative integrants of theological reflection. In view of this fact, and of the Marxist extraction of these elements, somebody may ask: Is this still *theo*logy? Assmann responds, firstly, that every theology obeys, in fact, an assumed situation, whether consciously or not, by means of some ideological option; and, secondly:

> . . . the criteria for a good theology are not any more strictly theological, just as the criteria for an effective love of God belong to the historical and human order of the neighbor, i.e., to the order of the nondivine. In fact, just as the *divine* dimension in the love of the neighbor is the God-reference in the neighbor, so the *theological* in the reflection on the historical praxis is present in the dimension of faith. If the divine, therefore, can only be found through the human, it is entirely logical that a Christian theology will find its ultimate theological character in the human references of history (p. 112).

Although it is not possible at this point to enter into greater detail, three consequences of this vision deserve to be mentioned: (1) It makes possible to unmask and denounce the false theologies that cover ideologically enslaving political options (theologies of the rich world, theologies of development, "third positions," etc.). (2) It helps to break the blocking of the Christian mind in dealing with questions such as the conflictive character of history, the problem of violence, and others.[6] (3) It brings to light a series of problems inherent in historical praxis which ideologies—the Marxist one, for instance—have ignored or refused to face because they lack categories to grapple with them: death, fellowship, sacrifice. Theology can make here a valuable contribution. But it will do it only insofar as it places itself within a concrete and real historical engagement. It is essential for this theology not to keep a "residuum" outside commitment, not to suppress all dualism between faith and historical praxis and—as I see it—between theological and ideological reflection.

Among the Protestants in Latin America, theological reflection is a new thing. They used to be satisfied with translations, reproductions, or adaptations of European or North American religious books. Lately, nevertheless, a certain creativity seems to have kindled in some Protestant quarters. We shall choose among these "first fruits" the man who has produced the first systematic exploration of the theme of liberation. Rubem Alves,[7] a Brazilian, has done a significant part of his work in the U.S.A. His books are published in English, and therefore available to the reader. There are significant similarities and differences between his thought and that of the Catholic theologians indicated in this chapter. Alves moves much more consistently in the world of North European and American thought. His partners in dialogue and his references are almost exclusively taken from this world. He tends to use the philosophy of language, rather than sociological or political sciences as the coordinates for his own theological construction. Finally, he gives considerable attention to the question of a biblical hermeneutics. (In this sense, he is closer to Segundo.)

The point of departure is, nevertheless, the same. At the beginning of his first book, he disclaims any attempt to have created "a new idea or hypothesis." "I have simply tried to explore critically the elements and possibilities of a language which some Christian groups have begun to speak." A language, at the same time, is not for Alves a purely superstructural creation. "It is an expression of how a community has programmed a solution to its existential problems." Behind a language, therefore, there is a community engaged in a praxis. Alves intends to study the significance of the language that the new "revolutionary" communities (or "communities of liberation") have begun to use. Historical praxis becomes also for Alves, consequently, the matrix of theological thought. In fact, referring to the Hebrew concept of truth,[8] he advocates a new understanding of *truth,* not as an abstract realm of ideas, but as "efficacious truth," as "action," as "the name given by a historical community to its historical deeds, which were, are, and will be efficacious in the liberation of man."

Where is this community? Alves extends the limits to include, to be sure, the third world, but also the poor and oppressed in the developed world: i.e., the black in the U.S.A. and protesting youth groups throughout the world. His critique of oppression is also centered more amply in the technological and repressive society which has emerged from capitalism than in the capitalist relations of production. To put it briefly: Marcuse rather than Marx provides the terms of his analysis. As a consequence human freedom (the possibility of creativity, man as subject) rather than justice is the dominant element in his view of liberation. This is not to say that he ignores the more "material" dimensions (a Brazilian could hardly do it!). But his work is more clearly located in this area.

Alves begins, therefore, with the existence of groups of Christians who are discovering this liberating vocation, and are starting to read the Bible and the doctrine of the Church in a new way, to speak a new language, which is born in a concrete historical experience but which, at the same time, recognizes itself as the language of the same historical community of the Old and New Testaments. The exploration of this language (and of the consciousness of the community which created and creates it) demands, logically, two perspectives: the one defined by the relation of the community to its present historical circumstances and the one defined by its "memory," i.e., the relation of the present community with the fellowship of faith in the past, reaching back to the Bible. Methodologically, Alves chooses two parameters: the language of the human quest for liberation, of the engagement with man's historical freedom, of the openness to the future, *humanist messianism* and the language of the experience of liberation of the community of faith, the language of the exodus, *messianic humanism*. In the critical convergence of these two foci, we will find the authentic project of liberation, the meaning of the community of faith, and at the same time the meaning of historical existence.

How do these two parameters converge? The answer is in their radically critical character, in their adamant denial of "that which is," in their refusal to be determined by precedent

75

and to be conformed to existing reality: "A new future will not be reached through the logic immanent in the facts given in the present state of things." In the theological realm, the experience of the exodus reflects this critical awareness. God manifests himself as the power of liberation who rejects the objective and subjective impossibility of liberation of the "given" condition of the Israelite tribes. For the Bible, God is not the eternally Present One who renders superfluous the movement of history or the eternal Reason who enables man to understand—and therefore to accept—things as they are, but the freedom which intervenes in history in order to prevent the past from determining the future. He is the freedom that impregnates history for the birth of a discontinuous possibility; he is the subverter of the status quo.

Neither messianic humanism nor humanistic messianism conceives the critical principle in isolation, as an end, but only as a necessary and intrinsic means in the creation of a future of freedom for man. Alves weaves through the whole fabric of the book, as a permanent theme, Paul Lehmann's happy expression: "to make and to keep human life human."[9] Toward this goal both movements converge—the humanist and the messianic. In one of the sections, Alves points out that liberation is at the service of life. God makes himself solidary with man; his freedom is freedom for the history of man. At this point, taking distance from the future-oriented thought of Moltmann and Bloch, with whom he is closely linked, our author inserts his theology in the present situation of oppression, in man's suffering. Liberation is not simply a history that breaks in from a future totally unconnected with the present: it is a project which springs from the protest born of the suffering of the present; a protest to which God grants a future in which man enters through his action.

Man's action, though, will not occur merely in the subjectivity of the individual—as in existentialism's flight from history—nor in the construction of a welfare society—as in the technological flight from freedom and consequently from what is human—but in *politics,* understood as human action carrying out a humanizing project in a historical future. Alves has polemicized with the fathers of modern Protestant theology for not having seen this. Barth in his transcendentalism, Bultmann in his existentialism and Moltmann in his "futurism," have submitted to languages which do not take human life and action seriously. Once the political language is adopted, a tension appears between the humanist and the messianic. For humanistic messianism, politics is an exclusively human possibility: man's liberation by man alone. For messianic humanism, there is a politics of God, which is manifested in the exodus: Israel is not merely conscious of having liberated itself, but of having been liberated; a future which was objectively and subjectively closed (because of Egypt's oppressive power and its own "slave consciousness") is broken open by a God who reveals himself as free from history (namely, from the determinisms of history) and for history. In acting in this way, God makes human politics possible, opens room for it, drives a wedge which precedes man's creative action. God as the future of freedom and freedom for the future makes the liberating project possible even in the most oppressive circumstances. Humanism, on the other hand, ends in despair and cynicism because oppression subjects the conscience and obliterates the horizon of freedom. Christian hope, far from taking the place of political action, invites and demands that action in the present, in favor of the oppressed, in the light and direction of the promised future. This is the language of the gospel. The community which enters this action, acquires this consciousness, and uses this language is God's people, in continuity with the experience of Israel and the New Testament—whether they stay within or more outside the visible ecclesiastical institutions. For an engagement with man's liberation and a pressing for God's future are the true marks of the Church.

The reader acquainted with recent European and American

theology may have felt somewhat puzzled as he was progressing through this chapter. He may have had the impression that he was treading on familiar ground, but things looked at times curiously different. The echoes of the voices of Barth, Bonhoeffer, Rahner, Moltmann, Metz, even of Lehmann, Shaull, and Cox met him every so often and were unmistakable. But they were pitched differently, modified, until they seemed almost different voices. Is there any way of accounting for this phenomenon? I shall try to begin answering this question by suggesting some clues for the interpretation of this theology.

The first has to do with the way in which theology refers to its subject. If theology—however it may be more precisely defined—has something to do with God and his action, it is evident that it cannot refer directly to its subject. Leaving aside the problem of a mystical experience, one must admit that language about God is necessarily analogical. This, which many of the Fathers knew, is today an accepted and rigorously investigated fact. In what realm of human experience and activity shall we find the categories for naming the themes of theology? Religion and metaphysics have traditionally provided the answer. But the world of religion and metaphysics has been growing increasingly dim during the last four centuries. Theology has consequently tried to articulate its knowledge in more decidedly anthropological terms, resorting to psychological or existential analysis. But in the last decades, converging lines of human experience and thought and of biblical research have pointed to the realm of history as the proper quarry for theological building material. Consequently, the sciences dealing with historical life—sociology, politics, the sciences of culture—have more and more provided the categories and articulations for theology. This double shift from the metaphysical to the anthropological and from the inner-personal to the public-historical marks the works of the European and American theologians we have just mentioned. Some of them, like Metz, Moltmann, or Cox, have explicitly argued for the use of this historical language and, more precisely, for a *political* transcription of the gospel. Here is the undeniable kinship with and indebtedness to these authors that our theologians manifest.

The option for a historical, political language has, nevertheless, been radicalized in Latin America, by bringing it down, not merely to the language and categories of a "general" analysis of historical existence, but to the concrete contents of our own social, cultural, political, and economic experience and to the categories that our own sociopolitical analysts have forged in order to grasp this experience. Thus, theological language has gained a painful concreteness which sounds strangely unfamiliar and perhaps irritating. "Terms which point to this sociopolitical infrastructure come in their own right into the language of the most rigorous theology," writes J.-L. Segundo, and he illustrates this with such terms as "conscientization, imperialism, international market, monopolies, social classes, developmentalism."[10] We shall discuss later on the legitimacy or otherwise of such a claim. It is enough, at the present point, to indicate some of its consequences.

The choice of a language is never a purely neutral or formal decision. In the very act, a realm of reality, or better said, a relation to reality is introduced as subject matter of theology. This is particularly so in the political case, when the categories chosen do not merely intend to describe human existence but to shape and transform it. A theology cast in political terms cannot satisfy itself with reformulating in a new way the theological heritage; it has to grapple with the dynamics of the language it uses. It has to concern itself with its relation to power. The words it uses belong to a context of militancy. The categories of analysis in which it casts its reflection are engaged categories and, as they gain a certain determinant power, the theologian cannot remain any more above the realm of political options. Latitudinarianism is dead: Latin American theol-

79

ogy becomes therefore a militant theology—a partisan theology, perhaps.

Such an option will certainly strike most academic theologians as strange. It will seem to lead to a sort of ideological and political captivity. Postponing a more careful analysis of this objection, we must nevertheless venture some answers. The first takes the form of a counter-question: Where is the theologian who has not made such an option, whether he knows it or not? Assmann, Segundo, Gutiérrez attack the attempt of such theologians as Küng, Metz, or Moltmann to remain at a nonpartisan level. The Latin Americans are constantly engaged in unmasking the ideologies smuggled in apparently neutral theologies. The words *apparently* or *unconsciously* lead into the second question and answer: What are the criteria for judging a theology's commitment? Today we know enough about language, thanks to structural analysis, to realize that the meaning of a language is determined not simply by the intention of the speaker but through the code or context of meanings which are already present and into which the pronounced word becomes inserted, independently of the speaker's intention. Words, for instance, which Moltmann and Metz use as clues, have their own meanings in terms of the ideological conflicts of the present. Unless they be specified in relation to a concrete world of references (the imperialist question, the class struggle, capitalism, and so forth) they will specify themselves through the cultural and political context in which they function. In Europe, for instance, they immediately are integrated into the developmentalist, technological, liberal ideology adopted by the Common Market and its orbit in relation to the third world. The question, therefore, is not what is intended with words, but how do they operate. And they always operate in a given direction. There are, from this point of view, no nonpartisan languages.

Another way of posing the same problem is to ask for the verifiability of a language. Once we resign reference to a metaphysical realm, a world of ideas in which theological categories have their referents, the only possibility is to relate a language to forms of conduct, to action, to a praxis. There is no direct access from words and meanings to a theological reality outside time and history. God can only be named through the reference to a concrete community of historical existence, in relation to which words define their meanings. This verifiability, to which we shall return, makes a Copernican change in theology (whether as a return to, or a betrayal of, the origin will occupy us later). Theology, as here conceived, is not an effort to give a correct understanding of God's attributes or actions but an effort to articulate the action of faith, the shape of praxis conceived and realized in obedience. As philosophy in Marx's famous *dictum,* theology has to stop explaining the world and to start transforming it. *Orthopraxis,* rather than orthodoxy, becomes the criterion for theology.

Finally, in such an understanding of the language and function of theology, there is no possibility of invoking or availing oneself of a norm outside praxis itself. This does not involve a rejection of the scriptural text or of tradition, but the recognition of the simple fact that we always read a text which is already incorporated in a praxis, whether our own or somebody else's. There is no possibility of extracting the text and projecting it objectively as a norm. There is only the possibility of criticism from within ourselves or in dialogue with others. This simple fact has somber, wide-ranging, practical consequences for hermeneutics (what are the conditions for this immanent criticism of one's own engaged praxis?) and for ecclesiology (how it this dialogue of antithetically committed "readings" related to the community of faith?). The elimination of a distinction of realms, which we saw in Gutiérrez, or the affirmation of one single history, to which many European theologians would also suscribe, proves to lead to some critical questions. If metaphysical reference is removed, and salvation history absorbed in an undifferentiated human history, how is the normative character of the "original events" of faith to be preserved? We face here a number of crucial problems. The modifications in the language and categories in theology reveal a more basic fact: we are being confronted by a new way of "doing theology." Gutiérrez's way of putting it is worth quoting:

> ... the theology of liberation offers us not so much a new theme for reflection as a *new way* of making theology. Theology as critical reflection on historical praxis is thus a liberating theology, a theology of the liberating transformation of the history of mankind and, therefore, also of that portion of it—gathered as *ecclesia*—which openly confesses Christ. [It is] a theology which does not limit itself to think the world, but which attempts to place itself as a moment of the process through which the world is transformed: opening itself—in the protest against the trodden dignity of man, in the struggle against the plunder of the immense majority of men, in the love which liberates, in the construction of a new, just and fraternal society—to the gift of God's Kindgom.[11]

NOTES

[1] There is already a vast amount of literature on "the theology of liberation." The reader will find an indication of bibliographical sources in the bibliography at the back of the book.

[2] Born in 1925, Juan Luís Segundo, Uruguayan Jesuit, with doctorates of theology and sociology from Louvain and Paris, is director of the "Pedro Fabbro Institute" of socio-religious research in Montevideo (Uruguay). A bibliography of his most important books will be found at the back of this book.

[3] Gera's theological production consists mostly of unpublished theological documents, frequently of great depth and scholarship, related to the concrete problems faced by the Church in the Argentine situation. In the summary presented here we will be drawing particularly from four essays, which we quote in the text by number and page: (I) "Fundamentaciones teológicas de la Acción por la Justicia y la Paz," *Primer encuentro regional de Justicia y Paz, cono sur* (Buenos Aires: undated, 9 pp.); (II) "La aparición del fenómeno político en el campo de reflexión de la teología," *ULAJE comparte* (Buenos Aires: Agosto de 1971), no. 5, pp. 1-7; (III) "La Iglesia debe comprometerse en lo político?" *Seminario Catequístico María Reina* (Buenos Aires: undated, 9 pp.); (IV) "La misión de la Iglesia y el presbítero a la luz de la

teología," *Pasos,* Santiago, Chile, no. 14 (August 14, 1972), 21 pp. Cf. also n. 2 in Chapter One.

⁴ Gustavo Gutiérrez is a Peruvian priest who has done his postgraduate theological studies in Europe. He serves as advisor to student movements in Lima and is an active participant in ONIS (see above, Chapter Three). His book *Teología de la Liberación* has been translated into several languages and is the best known and most comprehensive presentation of the new theological thought in Latin America. We quote from it, giving the pages in the English translation, but the version offered is ours.

⁵ Hugo Assmann is a Brazilian priest. He studied theology in Brazil and Europe and has served as assistant professor in Germany. His participation in the struggle for liberation has successively forced him out of Brazil, Uruguay, Bolivia, and lately Chile. He now teaches at the Department of Ecumenical Studies of the University of San José (Costa Rica, C.A.). Unless otherwise indicated, the quotations are from the first edition of his book *Opresión-Liberación.*

⁶ Assmann has particularly stressed this point and made some initial and very significant studies of the socio-psychological mechanisms of "blocking" and "unblocking." See his article "El cristianismo, su plusvalía ideológica y el costo social de la revolución socialista," in *Cuadernos de la Realidad Nacional* (Santiago, Chile: Universidad Católica, CEREN; April, 1972), no. 12, pp. 154-179.

⁷ Rubem Alves studied theology in Brazil and at Princeton Theological Seminary. His doctoral thesis has been published under the title *A Theology of Human Hope.* He has served as Study Secretary for Church and Society in Latin America and is at present professor of philosophy of religion at Sao Paulo University (Sao Paulo, Brazil). Unless otherwise indicated we quote from this book in the English edition.

⁸ Alves has developed this point, contrasting not only the idealist but also the technological understanding of truth with a critical, praxis-related thought and language in the article "Apuntes para un programa de reconstrucción en Teología," *Cristianismo y Sociedad* (Montevideo, 1969), no. 4, pp. 21 ff.

⁹ Paul L. Lehmann, *Ethics in a Christian Context* (New York: Harper & Row, 1963).

¹⁰ Juan L. Segundo, quoted by H. Assmann, *Opresión-Liberación,* p. 71.

¹¹ Gutiérrez, *A Theology of Liberation,* p. 15.

Part Two
CRITICAL REFLECTION

Chapter Five

Hermeneutics, Truth, and Praxis

The new theological consciousness is not without opposition inside Latin America. Serious objections have also been expressed outside our continent. "Our language is so new"— writes Segundo—"that to some it looks like a travesty of the gospel."[1] While the new Latin American theology is deeply polemical, it is not isolationist. Its spokesmen are aware of the problems raised by this new way of doing theology and are willing to discuss them. But they will refuse to be subject to the academic theology of the West as a sort of *norma normans* to which all theology is accountable. And they will reject a theological debate which proceeds as if abstracted from the total situation in which reflection takes place. In the chapters that follow we shall explore some of the questions raised in the theological dialogue which begins to develop across the chasm that divides the rich and the poor. We shall simply try to locate the questions and suggest lines along which they can be pursued. Obviously, they will be approached from the perspective of our own—Latin American—location. But hopefully it will be possible to suggest their correspondence with old and fundamental theological questions and motifs.

The "ideologization" of the gospel is perhaps the charge most frequently brought against this theology. In an acid criticism of the thought of ISAL, the Peruvian evangelical Pedro Arana concludes:

In the ideology of ISAL, God is translated by revolution; the people of God by the revolutionary hosts, and the Word of God by the revolutionary writings. Nobody will fail to see that all of this is Marxist humanism.[2]

The ghost of "German Christians" and their monstrous accommodation to Nazi ideology are frequently conjured in order to anathematize the theology of liberation. The problem is serious. It is not simply a question of some unfortunate or risky formulations of avant-garde or scandal-loving theologians, but of the very basis of the method of interpretation and the structure of theological reflection used in this theology. It appears as the hopeless prisoner of a hermeneutical circle, the spell of which it cannot break. The text of Scripture and tradition is forced into the Procrustean bed of ideology, and the theologian who has fallen prey of this procedure is forever condemned to listen only to the echo of his own ideology. There is no redemption for this theology, because it has muzzled the Word of God in its transcendence and freedom.

We shall see further on that the criticism is not without significance. In fact, it seems to me that our Latin American theology of liberation has not yet become sufficiently aware of the weight of this risk and consequently has not yet developed adequate safeguards against it. But before we undertake such a task it seems important to put the question in the right way, which, if I understand things correctly, is not primarily the cognitive level of understanding and interpretation, but the *historical* level of praxis and obedience; or to put it more precisely, the mutual relation and the unity of the two.

I shall try to indicate the problem by means of a brief story.[3] A young Puerto Rican professor of theology spent some time in prison for political reasons—demonstration against U.S. military experiments in his land. As he was trying to explain to other (non-Christian) fellow prisoners how his participation in this action was anchored in his Christian faith, one of them cut him short: "Listen, your faith does not mean a thing, because you can justify your political course of action and the man who put you in prison can do the same, appealing to the same truth." How can this objection be answered? There are two possible answers that we want to exclude. The first one would be: "This is the way I feel," "This is the way I decide," or "This is what Christianity means to me." There is no need to spend much time on this answer: it clearly places us in the quicksands of subjectivism and voluntarism, in which all objective historical contents either in Christianity or of the present are vacated. For this reason, most people would veer to a second answer: "There is an absolute Christian truth, or Christian principles, somehow enshrined in Scripture and/or in the pronouncements of the Church. But then, there are more or less imperfect *applications* of that truth." This answer expresses what could be called the classical conception of the relationship between truth and practice. Truth belongs, for this view, to a world of truth, a universe complete in itself, which is copied or reproduced in "correct" propositions, in a theory (namely, a contemplation of this universe) which corresponds to this truth. Then, in a second moment, as a later step, comes the application in a particular historical situation. Truth is therefore preexistent to and independent of its historical effectiveness. Its legitimacy has to be tested in relation to this abstract "heaven of truth," quite apart from its historicization.

It is this conception of truth that has come to a crisis in the theology which we are discussing. When Assmann speaks of the rejection of "any *logos* which is not the *logos* of a *praxis*"[4] or Gutiérrez writes about an "epistemological split,"[5] they are not merely saying that truth must be applied, or even that truth is related to its application. They are saying, in fact, that there is no truth outside or beyond the concrete historical events in which men are involved as agents. There is, therefore, no knowledge except in action itself, in the process of transforming the world through participation in history. As soon as such a formulation is presented, objections will be raised that (1) biblical truth is reduced to ethical action—the classical heresy of several forms of humanism, (2) the vertical dimension is swallowed in the horizontal, (3) this is the Marxist view of knowledge.

Before arriving at such judgments, we should raise at least two questions concerning the classical view. The first one is whether it corresponds to the biblical concept of truth. In this respect it will suffice to mention several converging lines in biblical scholarship and interpretation. Whatever corrections may be needed, there is scarcely any doubt that God's Word is not understood in the Old Testament as a conceptual communication but as a creative event, a history-making pronouncement. Its truth does not consist in some correspondence to an idea but in its efficacy in carrying out God's promise or fulfilling his judgment. Correspondingly, what is required of Israel is not an ethical inference but an obedient participation—whether in action or in suffering—in God's active righteousness and mercy. Faith is always a concrete obedience which relies on God's promise and is vindicated in the act of obedience: Abraham offering his only son, Moses stepping into the Red Sea. There is no question of arriving at or possessing previously some theoretical clue. There is no name of God to call forth—or to exegete—except as he himself is present in his power (i.e., his powerful acts). Again, the faith of Israel is consistently portrayed, not as a *gnosis*, but as a *way*, a particular way of acting, of relating inside and outside the nation, of ordering life at every conceivable level, which corresponds to God's own way with Israel. This background, so well attested in the Psalms, for instance, may explain Jesus' use of the word *way* to refer to himself. The motif, on the other hand, appears in parenetic contexts in Pauline literature. Faith is a "walking." It is unnecessary to point out that even the idea of knowledge and knowing has this active and participatory content.

This way of conceiving truth finds an explicit confirmation in the Johannine emphasis on "*doing* the truth." God's Word (his

Logos) is an incarnate word, a human flesh which has pitched its tent in history. Knowledge of such Logos is fellowship, participation in this new "life" which has been made available in the midst of the old "world." It is "a new birth." There is no way to this understanding through the mere exegetical exercise of the new teaching: "Why do you not understand what I say (*lalia*)? It is because you cannot bear to hear my word (*Logos*)" (John 8:43). One must be ready to enter actively into this relation, this life: only he who *does* the word will know the doctrine. The Johannine epistles work out the same theme relating the knowledge of God to the love of the brother. God is unknown unless man participates in his concrete life through love. There is here no minimizing of the historical revelation in Jesus Christ—quite the contrary, this is a critical test for the author. But this revelation is not an abstract theoretical knowledge but a concrete existence: the existence in love.[6]

The point could be much more elaborated in relation to other blocks of biblical writings. It seems clear enough that the classical conception can claim no biblical basis for its conceptual understanding of truth or for its distinction between a theoretical knowledge of truth and a practical application of it. Correct knowledge is contingent on right doing. Or rather, the knowledge is disclosed in the doing. Wrongdoing is ignorance. But, on the other hand, we can also ask whether this classical distinction is phenomenologically true? Is there, in fact, a theoretical knowledge prior to its application? It seems that both Scripture and social analysis yield the same answer: there is no such neutral knowledge. The sociology of knowledge makes abundantly clear that we think always out of a definite context of relations and action, out of a given praxis. What Bultmann has so convincingly argued concerning a *preunderstanding,* which every man brings to his interpretation of the text, must be deepened and made more concrete, not in the abstract philosophical analysis of existence but in the concrete conditions of men who belong to a certain time, people, and class, who are engaged in certain courses of action, even of Christian action, and who reflect and read the texts within and out of these conditions.

If these observations concerning the biblical understanding of truth and of the conditions of knowing are correct, as the phenomenological analysis also indicates from another perspective, several basic points emerge in relation to the question of hermeneutics. We indicate some of these points, which demand a careful examination.[7]

Every interpretation of the texts which is offered to us (whether as exegesis or as systematic or as ethical interpretation) must be investigated in relation to the praxis out of which it comes. At this point the instruments created by the two modern masters in the art of "suspecting," namely, Freud and Marx, are of great significance. Very concretely, we cannot receive the theological interpretation coming from the rich world without suspecting it and, therefore, asking what kind of praxis it supports, reflects, or legitimizes. Why is it, for instance, that the obvious political motifs and undertones in the life of Jesus have remained so hidden to liberal interpreters until very recently? Is this merely a regrettable oversight on the part of these scholars or is it—mostly unconscious, to be sure—the expression of the liberal ideological distinction of levels or spheres which relegates religion to the area of subjectivity and individual privacy? In a similar vein, Juan Luís Segundo finds the clue to the common image of a timeless and impersonal God not only in the speculative, philosophical influences which went into its creation, but in a view of a split life where man works and produces in an external, public, material area in order to "emerge to a zone identified as 'privacy'" in which he is supposed to realize his humanity. Is it not therefore quite understandable that God will be identified with this area, or even more, made the guarantor of it, and consequently distant from the world of outward, material, history?[8] When Freud and Marx denounce such a God as an ideological projection through which we disguise our inability to deal with our own human, historical, and material reality, they are providing the tools for a purification of our theological hermeneutics. This, in turn, opens the door to a reconception of the theological heritage.

Even more important is the question of the verifiability of Christianity—or of the interpretation of Christianity as it operates historically. The problem of verifiability cannot be evaded; it has always confronted Christianity. But since the second century it has been approached apologetically as the question of the rationality of the Christian faith. Theological systems have changed according to the changes in the philosophical systems which at a given time offered the framework for the explanation of ultimate reality. It was crucial to show that the Christian faith made sense in terms of such frameworks of interpretation. Three facts, at least, force us today out of this type of verification. On the one hand, the demise of metaphysics has made all reference to this trans-reality of human and worldly things largely irrelevant. We can no longer find in such a world a valid correlate for our theological language. Secondly, we have now the instruments for assessing and analyzing the historical impact of the Christian faith. Since socio-analytical sciences have uncovered the concrete historical dynamics of Christianity (i.e., the relation of Protestantism to capitalism, the relation of social *anomie* and the growth of sects, and so on) and since structural analysis permits us to expose the ideological functions of religious language, we can no longer measure the proclamation and witness of the Church in terms of the conceptual contents of its doctrine, disclaiming as "spurious" or "incidental" the so-called consequences of such doctrine. The meaning of Christianity cannot be abstracted from its historical significance. Words—whatever the speaker may intend—communicate in relation to a code that is historically defined, and this code has not been created out of ideas but of the total experience of a given time and people—an experience which incorporates the actual historical impact of the Christian faith. Finally, the biblical witness itself will not let us find refuge in such a conceptual firmament. Its references are always time- and place-bound. It speaks of events that took place, take place, and will take place in history, in the world of men, events that can be dated in relation to Pharaoh, Nebuchadnezzar, or Augustus. God himself is, to be sure, the main actor in these events. But there is no attempt to infer God's action from some previously ascertainable project or idea. Rather, his character is to be known in his acts (which, to be sure, are not without their "word," but a word verified in the act).

Finally, both the criticism and the introduction of the criterion of historical verifiability introduce into the hermeneutical task new areas and instruments. We are not concerned with establishing through deduction the consequences of conceptual truths but with analyzing a historical praxis which claims to be Christian. This critical analysis includes a number of operations, which are totally unknown to classical theology. Historical praxis overflows the area of the subjective and private. If we are dealing with acts and not merely with ideas, feelings, or intentions, we plunge immediately into the area of politics, understood now in its broad sense of public or social. Billy Graham, the South African Reformed Church, Martin Luther King, or "Christians for socialism" do not confront us primarily as a system of ideas or a theological position but as historical agents acting in certain directions and with certain effects which are objectively possible to determine. The area of research is the total society in which these agents are performing; economic, political, and cultural facts are as relevant to a knowledge of these praxes as the exegesis of their pronouncements and publications. Their Christianity must be verified in relation to such questions as imperialism, apartheid, integration, self-determination, and many other sociopolitical magnitudes.

It is obvious that such an analysis brings with it the tools of sociopolitical sciences. A recent study of Chilean Pentecostalism, for instance, researches the mechanisms of authority and control operative in these communities in relation to secular models prevailing in the society: the *caudillo* (leader), the paternalistic landowner, the democratic model. It compares the behavior of the Pentecostal groups with the normal class behavior of Chilean society (of the same classes). It assesses attitudes toward money, work, politics with reference to classic Protestant models. Out of these data a picture emerges of an interpretation of the gospel *as it really* works itself out in history in this particular time and place. The result of this research, though, does not leave us simply with a sum of facts; it discloses a (more or less coherent, or partially modified) unified perception of the world, i.e., an ideology.[9] Hermeneutics in this new context means also an identification of the ideological frameworks of interpretation implicit in a given religious praxis. It is important to point out, in this respect, that such discernment of an ideology implicit in a theological or religious praxis does not necessarily imply the intention of the person or group in question to uphold or promote such ideology. One could even venture to say that, in most cases, people are themselves unaware of it. Their words and actions may intend something else. But in the context of a given situation they may in *fact* be supporting and buttressing a certain political and/or economic line and, therefore, functioning, in the wider context of the total society, as ideological justification of such lines.[10] It is important to make this distinction because it has to do with the concrete historical character of Christian acts and pronouncements. This makes possible—and this is nothing new in the area of doctrinal development—that a position taken at one point in history may acquire in a different setting an ideological connotation.

In the same context, it is important to recognize that this identification of the ideology implicit in a given historical praxis does not as such disqualify it. Any course of action which keeps a certain coherence implies a unified perspective on reality, an explicit or implicit project. Ideology, in this sense, has also a positive meaning; it is the instrument through which our Christian obedience gains coherence and unity. It is so, though, provided that it be always brought to consciousness and critically examined both in terms of the gospel and of the scientific analysis of reality. As soon as we make such a formulation, we are faced with several problems, which it is now necessary to broach.

If it be true that every form of praxis articulates—consciously or unconsciously—a view of reality and a projection of it, an analysis and an ideology, this means that reflection on this praxis must necessarily raise the question of the rightness or inadequacy of such analysis and ideology. This is a complex problem to which we cannot expect to find an unobjectionable answer. But the question is unavoidable. It is at this point that the theology of the most history-conscious European and American theologians seems to us to fail. They grant that faith emerges as a historical praxis. Moreover, they grant the political (i.e., public) character of this praxis. But then, they want to remain at some neutral or intermediate level in which there is no need to opt for this or that concrete political praxis, i.e., to assume a particular analysis and a particular ideological projection. We have already seen that such an attempt is self-deceptive. The opposite position, which we adopt, brings with it a particular risk. Nobody will claim, in fact, that his analysis of social, political, and economic reality is more than a rational exercise, open to revision, correction, or rejection. It is in this sense that we incorporate the Marxist analysis of society. The point is of great importance and the source of many misunderstandings. Our assumption of Marxism has nothing to do with a supposedly abstract or eternal theory or with dogmatic formulae—a view which is not absent in certain Marxist circles—but with a scientific analysis and a number of verifiable hypotheses in relation to conditions obtaining in certain historical moments and places and which, properly modified, corrected, and supplemented, provide an adequate means to grasp our own historical situation (insofar, moreover, as it is closely related and significantly shaped by the model originally analyzed).

It seems to me that there is no small confusion in Christian revolutionary circles because of an ambivalence or oscillation in the Marxist self-understanding. Dialectical materialism and historic materialism are conceived by some as a metaphysical theory, an absolute philosophical formulation. As such, it seems to enter immediately in conflict with the Christian faith in God. There are, therefore, a number of Christians who, while unreservedly taking up the cause of the oppressed, refuse (or at least take with great reticence) elements of the Marxist analysis such as the class struggle, the role of the proletariat, and other elements. The problem is that instead they usually assert "ethical principles" which, lacking a rigorous historical mediation, not infrequently end up in frustration, inability to act or different forms of reformism. On the other extreme, and falling prey to the same error, not a few Christians have embraced Marxist ideology—understood in the absolute terms indicated above—with a sort of religious fervor. This, in turn, results in a total loss of faith or in the surrender of the historical contents of the Christian gospel. There can be no doubt as to the sincerity of many of these people. They may in fact be much closer to the Kingdom than most of their orthodox opponents. But it seems that neither alternative is satisfactory: we cannot accept the either/or of political naïveté and inefficacy or the surrender of Christian identity.

A third and difficult way seems to be open. It begins by recognizing that a concrete and specific form of analysis of reality is necessary for Christian obedience (not only in general but in specific and particular political, social, and economic terms). It further recognizes that such an analysis cannot be neutral, uncommitted (supposedly objective), because such so-called descriptive views (witness sociological functionalism) take present reality as normative and consequently are simply tools for the preservation of the status quo. A really objective view of historical reality requires significant hypotheses relating to "constancies" or (with all necessary *caveats*) "laws" to direct our action in history. For some of us Marxism can be assumed at this level. It is an analysis of the way in which socio-economic-political reality functioned at a certain point in history (the stage of capitalism which Marx observed). This analysis was significantly projected into an hypothesis concerning the relation of human history (and all its achievements) to the process of producing material goods. As an hypothesis it has been tested against our knowledge of the past and against conditions obtaining later on and in different situations. It has been refined, supplemented, or developed. But it seems to many of us that it has proved, and still proves to be, the best instrument available for an effective and rational realization of human possibilities in historical life. A Marxist praxis is both the verification and the source of possible correction of the hypothesis.

Admittedly, Marxism does not behave as the cool rational entity we have described. It is frequently possessed by an apostolic zeal, a dogmatic certainty and a messianic fervor the causes of which we cannot discuss here, although we shall return in Chapter Seven to an aspect of this question. We have here a particular form of the old problem of the relation of the Christian faith to the form of rationality in and through which it shapes its obedience and reflection. Philosophical systems used in the past seemed to be somewhat removed from actual practice and confined to speculation while Marxism proposes a form of action as the rationality corresponding to history. We have already seen that this distinction is superficial both in terms of the ideological contents of metaphysical speculation and the historical demand of the Christian faith. When we speak of assuming Marxist analysis and ideology at this point, there is therefore no sacralization of an ideology, no desire to "theologize" sociological, economic, or political categories. We move totally and solely in the area of human rationality—in the realm where God has invited man to be *on his own*. The only legitimate question is therefore whether this analysis and this projection do in fact correspond to the facts of human history. If they do, or to the extent that they do, they become *the unavoidable historical mediation* of Christian obedience.

Once we have located the sociopolitical and even (to some extent) ideological problems at this rational, historical level, the question remains whether this dimension is, so to speak, autonomous or somehow related to or "overdetermined" by other considerations. Posed in this way, the question might lead to misunderstanding, as if we would fall again into the scheme of some supratemporal moral or religious truth which then is applied through a rational, scientific method. The desire to eradicate this fatal mistake has led most of the Latin American theologians to whom we have referred to neglect this question or to dismiss it rather summarily. The problem, nevertheless, will not rest. Christian obedience, understood to be sure as a historical praxis, and therefore incarnate in a historical (rational, concrete) mediation does, nevertheless, incorporate a dimension which, using christological language, can never be separated from but neither can it be confused with the historical mediation. In other terms, how are the original events (or the "germinal" events as it would perhaps be more accurate to call them), namely, God's dealings with Israel, the birth, life, death, and resurrection of Jesus, the hope of the Kingdom— how are they determinative in this single, synthetical fact that we call the historical praxis of a Christian? If we are condemned to remain silent on this point, we are really resigning any attempt to speak of such praxis as *Christian* obedience.

We are just at the beginning of the historical praxis of Christian obedience that will help us to reflect on this problem. We will know as we do. Some considerations can, nevertheless, be advanced on the basis of the experience we already have, both in our own situation and in the tradition of the Christian community. The first remark is that this question is closely connected with the revolutionary need to criticize one's own praxis from within in order to re-project it in a deeper, more significant, and more effective way. Such criticism must be done from within in a double sense. On the one hand, it must be done in the context of active engagement, in relation to the real questions which are posed in the praxis itself. On the other hand, it should deepen and push further the theory which is incorporated in such praxis. This means in the context of our discussion at least two things. Negatively, that theology cannot claim to have some "pure kerygmatic truths or events," unengaged, or uncompromised in a concrete historical praxis, from where we can judge the concrete Christian obedience of a person or a community. All we have today in Latin America are reactionary, reformist, or revolutionary engagements, and therefore reactionary, reformist, or revolutionary readings of what we have called "germinal events of the Christian faith." Significant and fruitful self-criticism or dialogue can only take place when we consciously assume our own praxis and reflect from within it—or are converted to another. We cannot, therefore, take too seriously the frequent warnings and admonitions coming from European and (to a lesser extent) American theologians against our "ideological biases" as if they were speaking from some sort of ideologically aseptic environment.

But there is also a positive consequence of the same fact. Within the historical mediation of our Christian obedience, i.e., the struggle for liberation in the terms that have been defined, there is an ideological projection (now in a positive sense) which provides the terms for a significant criticism of our praxis. The social (collective) appropriation of the means of production, the suppression of a classist society, the de-alienation of work, the suppression of a slave consciousness, and the reinstallation of man as agent of his own history are the theoretical hypotheses on the basis of which revolutionary praxis is predicated. They become, therefore, *intrinsic tests* for such praxis. A consistent engagement demands a constant criticism in these terms.

It is not for us to say whether a Christian is in a better position to exercise that engaged criticism. This will be seen concretely in experience, or not at all. But it is possible to say, I think, that a Christian is called to do it, at least on two accounts. The first, to which we shall return, is the nature of the Christian kerygma itself. The second is the fact that, as a Christian, he has no self-image to preserve, no need to be justified by the blamelessness of his action, no value to attach to achievement beyond its significance for the neighbor, no claim to make on the basis of rightness. A Christian can offer his praxis to the fire of criticism totally and unreservedly on the trust of free grace just as he can offer his body totally and unreservedly in the hope of the resurrection. That so many nonbelievers do these things and so many Christians do not belongs to the mystery of grace and the mystery of evil. But the fact that this freedom is offered to faith at every moment is the very center of the gospel.

The mention of the Christian kerygma brings us to a final point which deserves our attention. We have said that there are only engaged readings of the Scripture, the kerygma, the story of the founding and generative events of the faith. But are they *readings* or only arbitrary *inventions*? The question is by no means academic for a Christian whose faith is rooted in Jesus Christ, who "has come in the flesh" and not in some Gnostic myth which can be reinvented at every new occasion. It is therefore decisive for an obedience that claims to be Christian obedience, the discipleship of that Christ, and not a new law or man-made ordinance.

The Scripture itself offers illustrative instances of engaged readings of the germinal events, for example, from the contexts in which the Lord's resurrection is presented in the New Testament. A careful and cautious exegete like the Swiss P. Bonnard indicates that "when the New Testament speaks of the resurrection of Jesus . . . it does not merely say that he has risen; it says *a number of things* which can be grouped . . . around six subjects." He then proceeds to indicate these various things that are said: "all will rise!"; "Christ is risen for our justification"; "we have risen with him"; "powers and dominations have been defeated"; "the risen one is the one who died"; "the Lord is present." In every case, as Bonnard himself indicates, these texts "are bearers of a present word." A careful study of the texts shows that "present word" is not understood merely as a consequence of the resurrection, a deduction from it, far less "an application" of the truth of the resurrection. In every case, it is the historical fact of the resurrection itself which is present and active in the second term of the message. In other words, the resurrection of Jesus *is* itself (and not merely means or causes) our resurrection, our justification, the defeat of the powers, the power of his death, the general resurrection, the active presence of Christ.[11] Is it altogether absurd to reread the resurrection today as the death of the monopolies, the liberation from hunger, or a solidary form of ownership?

Whether a reading of such events as the resurrection is arbitrary or not cannot be a purely subjective or situational judgment. When we say that, for the New Testament, the resurrection is read as one of several things, it is important to remark that we are really talking about the resurrection. At this point, with Barth, and contrary to Bultmann, we must reject any reduction to an "Easter faith" (or the equivalent in relation to other events). These events, and consequently the kerygma in which they come to us, are present in our reading in the full weight of their objective historicity as well as in the full efficacy of their dynamism. For this reason, theological hermeneutics cannot forgo the effort to gain access to the text by means of the critical (historical, literary, traditio-historical, linguistic) instruments which the sciences of interpretation have created. In this respect our theology must battle on two fronts. One—about which our theologians are very perceptive—is the criticism of the ideological premises of the Western sciences of interpretation. Even a cursory reading of the history of interpretation in European theology since the eighteenth century leaves little doubt in this respect. "Scientific," "historical," or "objective" exegesis reveals itself as full of ideological presuppositions. On the other hand, this battle of interpretations is not without a positive balance insofar as it has unmasked previous ideological readings and has helped us to liberate the text for a new and creative obedience. While the more significant Latin American theologians avail themselves continually of such study, they tend to minimize its theological significance. Their insistence on "present obedience" as the only legitimate reading of the biblical text is certainly quite justified. It is the first and most important thing that must be said. But we should not overlook the fact that the text opens itself for this present reading not in spite of its concrete, local, and *dated* historicity but because of it. To be sure, this affirmation opens the question of a double location of the texts and the threat of a new dualism. To this question we shall return in the last two chapters. At this point, and anticipating to a certain extent the conclusions to be reached later on, we must insist that the penetration of the original historicity of the biblical events is basic for its present demand and efficacy. Consequently, however questionable and imperfect, the critical use of the instruments that help us to reach a better understanding of this historicity is indispensable for a reflection on our Christian obedience today. Through these means we reach what Professor Casalis has called "a hermeneutical circulation" (over against the famous "hermeneutical circle" of the Bultmannians) between the text in its historicity and our own historical reading of it in obedience.[12]

Is the path of this circulation in any way verifiable? In other words, can the correlation between the text in its own historicity and our own historical reading of it be in any way controlled, verified, or falsified? The problem is as old as interpretation itself and can be clearly illustrated from the New Testament history of tradition itself. There is no point here in rehearsing the different forms in which such correlation has been found throughout history. But it seems important to define at least the limits within which a legitimate answer may be found. In the first place, let us underline again the fact that this reading is always a synthetic act, or, as the New Testament puts it, "a discernment in the Spirit," which has been promised to the faithful community. Obedience is not found as the conclusion of a syllogism but in the prophetic word of discernment received in faith. This prophecy is only partially justified theologically or even historically. Its final justification is eschatological, as the New Testament makes abundantly clear. Secondly, we cannot expect a direct historical correspondence, either in the form of law—witness the miscarriage of the Calvinist attempt at Geneva or the "enthusiasts" throughout history —or as precedent. This is the reason why, significant as they are, the attempts to derive direct political conclusions (either revolutionary or pacifist) from the ambivalent relation of Jesus to the Zealots, seems to me a dangerous short cut.

In order to avoid these short cuts we can rely on two mediations. One is the reading of the direction of the biblical text, particularly of the witness of the basic, germinal events of the faith. They seem, in fact, to point, in their integrity and coherence, to certain directions which such concepts as liberation, righteousness, shalom, the poor, love help us to define. The scope of these mediating concepts must always be searched in the historical elucidation, the progressive historicization, and the mutual complementation of the biblical text. The other mediation, on which we have already commented, is the determination of the historical conditions and possibilities of our present situation, as discovered through rational analysis. The correlation of the historical and conceptual mediations can offer us, not certainly a foolproof key to Christian obedience, but a significant framework for it.

On the basis of such an understanding of faithfulness to the revelation a man in the situation we described at the beginning of the chapter can say not, "My enemies and myself draw different possible conclusions from the same truth," or "This is the way I feel" but, "This is Christian obedience" and consequently "repression and imperialism are disobedience and heresy." This is certainly a dangerous answer. But so has every confessing decision that the Church has dared throughout history been dangerous. Obedience is always a risk.

NOTES

[1] Segundo, *De la Sociedad a la Teología,* p. 7.

[2] Pedro Arana, in the theological colloquium on "The Authority of the Bible" of the *Asociación Teológica Evangélica Latinoamericana,* which met in Cochabamba (Bolivia) in December, 1971. But it is interesting to note the growing concern of this evangelical lay theologian with a genuinely evangelical and engaged approach to the social and political questions. Cf. "Ordenes de la creación y responsabilidad social," in *Fe cristiana y Latinoamerica hoy,* ed. C. René Padilla (Buenos Aires: Ediciones Certeza, 1974), pp. 169–184 and even more in "La Liberación," a series of outlines for Bible study reproduced in *Pasos,* no. 53 (June 4, 1973).

[3] The story was told by Prof. Luis N. Rivera Pagán, from the "Seminario Unido" of Rio Piedras, Puerto Rico, at a meeting on liberation and theology in Buenos Aires, June, 1971.

[4] Assmann, *Opresión-Liberación,* p. 87.

[5] Gustavo Gutiérrez, *Praxis de Liberación y Fe Cristiana* (Lima: Centro de Documentación MIEI-JECI, Apartado 3564, 1973), p. 16.

[6] The Mexican Jesuit J.-L. Miranda has published a very penetrating exegetical study of this concept in Johannine literature, *El ser y el Mesías* (Salamanca: Ediciones Sígueme, 1973). Cf. also the work of the Spanish biblicist José M. Diez Alegría, *Yo creo en la esperanza* (Bilbao: Desclée de Brouwer, 1972), pp. 68–87.

[7] Some further observations and illustrations in my article, "Marxist critical tools: are they helpful?" in *Movement* (London: Student Christian Movement Press), no. 15, "The Politics of Bible Study," May, 1974.

[8] *Nuestra idea de Dios,* chap. II (E.T., pp. 66 ff.).

[9] Christian Lalive d'Epinay, *Haven of the Masses: A Study of the Pentecostal Movement in Chile* (London: Lutterworth, 1969).

[10] See the discussion in Chapter One on "colonial" and "neocolonial" Christianity in Latin America.

[11] P. Bonnard, "Quelques récits évangéliques relatifs au Réssuscité", in "Cahiers Bibliques" of *Foi et Vie* (January-February, 1970), no. 1, pp. 29-59.

[12] Perhaps the best discussion of this hermeneutical method as well as illustrations of its practice will be found in the book of the Argentine Old Testament scholar José Severino Croatto, *Liberación y Libertad: Pautas Hermenéuticas* (Buenos Aires: Ediciones Mundo Nuevo, 1973).

Chapter Six

Love, Reconciliation, and Class Struggle

In a book clearly directed against "Christians for socialism," the Chilean Guillermo Blanco denounces *The Gospel according to Judas* (the title of the book) which has turned the great commandment of Christ into: "Hate one another." With scathing irony he ridicules the "new gospel":[1]

> Forward!
> Go and teach to use the machine gun;
> Resist evil, smite the foolish one on both cheeks;
>   If you forgive men their faults, you will slow down the historical process;
>   Pray for your enemies only once you have efficiently killed them off;
>   Take your gun and follow me;
> . . . .

With less sarcasm but no less passion the Chilean Archbishop Primate warned shortly before the meeting: "Christianity is reduced to a revolutionary class struggle. . . .Christians are launched into the struggle for a Marxist revolution."[2] The contradiction between violence and class struggle on the one hand and the gospel of reconciliation and love on the other is emphasized both in official ecclesiastical pronouncements and in the conservative and liberal polemics against Marxism. The mere mention of these two sources suggests that several questions are here involved—socio-analytic, theological, and ideological. To sort out these problems, avoiding the pitfall of ideological demagoguery on the one hand and of domesticating the radical demand of love of the gospel on the other, requires more time and ability than we have at our disposal. But it is necessary to offer, at least, some preliminary remarks in order to clear the ground for a genuine discussion of the question. This is what we intend to do in this chapter.

"Christians for socialism" use the concept of class struggle in several contexts. In the description of the existing situation, it is recognized as a fact. As such, nevertheless, it is not a brute fact of nature; it is a process through which the oppressed discover their identity and strength and consciously assume the struggle. At this point, the struggle can be characterized as an instrument of liberation—the oppressed realize that it is only as they assert the conflict and carry it to its radical resolution that they will be able to wrest power from the hands of the oppressor and therefore to free themselves. The outcome of the struggle—and its intended aim—is not, nevertheless, a new oppression, a simple inversion of the relations of power, but the suppression of oppression, and therefore the elimination of the struggle. In other terms, class struggle is not seen as a permanent feature of human existence and history but as an evil, triggered by the oppressive character of the present economic (social and political) system; an evil that we must try to overcome by the elimination of this system. The struggle—often with a measure of violence—is inextricably woven into the revolutionary process but can in no way be idolized or hypostatized as an element of nature.[3]

This is no doubt a more or less typical Marxist analysis. As such, it frequently evokes in the Christian a critical reaction. The idea of confrontation, struggle, and violence seem particularly repugnant to the Christian conscience. Before dealing with the area of ethical questions we must, nevertheless, dwell briefly on the concept of class. The phenomenon of classes in society is analyzed by Marx in relation to the way in which people relate to the productive process, particularly in the capitalist form of organizing production. It is well known that Marx finds the main distinction hinging on whether a man owns the means of production or whether he has to sell his labor to those who own them, i.e., the capitalist and the proletarian. Marx and his followers are, of course, aware that this particular configuration of classes is dependent on the existing forms of the capitalist economy, and therefore cannot be projected back to other societies. Moreover, they are aware that even in the capitalist industrial societies several forms of production and consequently different forms of social organization coexist and therefore that there are groups and segments of society that do not fit neatly into this dominant pattern. One could add that tribal societies in Africa or ethnic groups in Latin America as well as changes in the structure of capitalist production pose complex problems which may require rethinking certain elements in the Marxist conception of class. Both Marxist and non-Marxist sociologists are aware of these questions and there is at present a very significant literature dealing with the problem. There is no need for us to belabor this point. We are here dealing with the always provisional results of a scientific investigation. As such, a Christian need not accept it or question it except in terms of its scientific verifiability.

There are, nevertheless, two theological questions which deserve to be mentioned. The first has to do with Marx's point of departure (whether itself a result of his scientific analysis or not is at this point a moot question), namely, that man is to be basically and radically understood as a worker, as the being who appropriates, transforms, and humanizes the world through his work and who himself comes to his own identity, becomes man through this same work. If this is so, it is only to be expected that the forms of relationships and organizations in which man works will be the privileged means for understanding human life and society and that changes in one area will be closely related to changes in the other. Christian anthropology, on the other hand, has traditionally sought to understand man in terms of his intellectual, moral, and spiritual endowment or, in a more dynamic way, in terms of his relations to himself (self-understanding), to his neighbor, and to God. The theological understanding of man, therefore, has been predominantly—if not exclusively—philosophical, cultural, and religious. To such an approach, Marxist anthropology naturally smacks of materialism. Such an accusation is very widespread in Christian circles. But one may wonder whether it does not rest on a twofold misunderstanding. On the one hand, it reads Marx in terms of a mechanistic determinism which would see the spiritual life of man as a mere reflex of material conditions. There is no doubt that some Marxist thinkers, and particularly many popularizers, have amply justified such interpretation. In Marx himself, and in the best contemporary interpreters, the dialectical relations of material and cultural conditionings are much more subtly and carefully assessed. It may, nevertheless, be necessary to challenge and correct even more drastically Marx's conception at this point. I am, at the same time, more concerned with the other misunderstanding: the theological substitution of an idealist for the biblical understanding of man. Whether one deals with the creation stories, with the law, or with the prophetic message, there seems to be in the Bible no relation of man to himself, to his neighbor, or even to God which is not mediated in terms of man's *work*. His dignity is located in his mission to subdue and cultivate the world. His worship is related to the fulfillment of a law in which the whole realm of his economic and political activity is taken up (and not to an image or idol in which he could find a private and direct access to the deity).

In the debate concerning voluntary work on Sundays, Professor Sergio Arce, of Cuba, has made some very significant points in this regard:

The fact that our Lord was resurrected the first day of the week sanctifies, once and for all, those six days which in the law of Moses were ordained for work. In that way, all legalistic "holiness" is withdrawn from the Sabbath day (the day of rest) by the power of the resurrection of our Lord. At the same time, each day of work, as the first day of the week, acquires a sacramental character, no longer now as a thing of the first eon or of the primary activity of God-in-this-world, but as something fulfilled by the new eon—by the Kingdom of heaven—and as a reconciling element.[4]

If this is true, the idealist inversion means a serious distortion. (Is it purely fortuitous that this idealist interpretation should have been developed by Greek philosophers living in an aristocracy of idleness in which manual work was confined to slaves?) To trace the consequences of such inversion in the understanding of sin, repentance, the relation of faith and obedience, and many other basic theological subjects is in itself a major theological project which claims urgent attention. A Christianity which has given up the mediation of work and the world as a constituent core of faith and can only reintroduce it later at a secondary, derivative level can only falsify both the gospel and man's most authentic experience. It can only lead to reducing redemption to a parody lived out in the realm of ideas (doctrine) or of subjectivity (intention or feeling) instead of the real world of creation; it can only be an opiate of the people!

At the same time, it must be said that, while the Marxist righting of the idealist inversion has allowed Christians to recover the biblical view of man, we are also forced to move beyond it. Marxism has understood the alienated character of work in our capitalist society, in which man is estranged from his work; work is objectified as something alien to him and bought through a salary. There is a striking similarity between this view and the Pauline rejection of "the works of the law" in which man's actions are also objectified as something "valuable in themselves," apart from the doer and the neighbor, as a "work" which can be merchandised in order to buy "justification." The work of faith, on the other hand, is never objectified—it is the believer himself in action in terms of love. The

Christian will, therefore, understand and fully join the Marxist protest against the capitalist demonic circle of work-commodity-salary. But out of the justification by faith alone, he will have to ask whether alienation does not have deeper roots than the distortions of the capitalist society, even in the mysterious original alienation, in man's denial of his humanity (his attempt to know outside the relation of trust and work) which we call sin. This question, nevertheless, can only be asked in the context of a service (a *leitourgeia,* an *abodah,* a service, and a work which are at the same time worship) freely rendered, a work done "out of faith," outside the realm of worth and reward, in the anticipation of the realm of creative love which is the Kingdom!

If the biblical view of man's humanity as realized in work is recovered, and at the same time we are aware of the distortion introduced by sin into the life of society, the existence of classes and their conflict emerges as a possible major category for our understanding of history; a possible one, I say, because we must be concerned here with empirical observation and its interpretation and not with a philosophical or theological axiom. "Class" is a sociological concept and must be verified as such. All we have tried to indicate in the preceding pages is that the view of man which emerges in the Marxist discussion of class—namely, man as worker—is also fundamental for a biblical anthropology. Another significant element appears in relation to the discussion of class: the biblical concept of "the poor." A number of studies have appeared recently, particularly in connection with the emphasis in Roman Catholic circles on "a Church of the poor." The result of biblical research on this point is aptly summarized by Gustavo Gutiérrez.[5] The notion of poverty in the Scriptures is an ambivalent one. On the one hand it designates the weak, the destitute, the oppressed, and is as such "a scandalous situation" which must be redressed. On the other hand it indicates "spiritual childhood," humility before God, and as such it is a—perhaps *the*—basic

111

virtue. When poverty has the former meaning, we find an unanimous prophetic protest against it. "For the prophets," concludes the Dutch scholar Van der Ploëg, "poverty was never a neutral thing. When they spoke about it, it was in order to protest against the oppression and injustice of the rich and powerful." Poverty is not a hazard of fortune or a fact of nature but the result of certain people's greed and injustice. It is intolerable because it contradicts the very purpose of God's mighty act of deliverance—to rescue his people from the slavery of Egypt. It robs man of his humanity as a steward and transformer of the world and therefore it contradicts the mandate of creation. Finally, it breaks human solidarity, and consequently it destroys fellowship among men and with God. Poverty, in this sense, is a scandalous fact which must be eliminated. God himself is engaged in the struggle against it; he is clearly and unequivocally on the side of the poor.

On the other slope of the vocabulary of poverty is the idea of a faithful "remnant" which does not yield to the apostasy of God's chosen people. They suffer contempt, persecution, and oppression but place their trust in God's promise and wait for the manifestation of his righteousness. This is the poverty referred to in the Matthew version of the first Beatitude. The question is: Is there a summit in which these two slopes of the notion of poverty find their unity? Gutiérrez finds an answer in the Pauline text: "For you know the grace of our Lord Jesus Christ that, though he was rich, yet for your sake he became poor, so that by his poverty you might become rich" (2 Cor. 8:9). Christian poverty, the believer's humility before God, incarnates itself in the solidarity with the poor and oppressed. "There is no question of idealizing poverty but, on the contrary, it must be assumed for what it is—as an evil, in order to protest against it and to fight for its abolition," writes Gutiérrez. "Christian poverty," he concludes, "as an expression of love, is solidary *with the poor* and it is a protest *against poverty.*"[6]

Now, is there a transition from the biblical idea of the poor to the Marxist view of an oppressed class? Can the Christian call to solidarity with the poor and the revolutionary convocation to class struggle be equated? There seems to be both a genuine and sound discernment but also some dangerous misunderstandings and short-cutting in these identifications. As to the first, there seems to be no serious possibility to argue on biblical and theological grounds against Karl Barth's dictum: "God always takes his stand unconditionally and passionately on this side and on this side alone: against the lofty and in behalf of the lowly. . . ."[7] The misunderstandings arise from an insufficient recognition of the necessary analytical mediations between the Marxist category of the "proletarian class" and the biblical one of "the poor." This latter one—insofar as it refers to the oppressed and disinherited—is a prescientific, simply empirical designation arising out of direct observation of a situation of oppression and injustice. When Christians in Latin America (or elsewhere) denounce the hard and moving realities of hunger, unemployment, premature death, exploitation, repression, and torture, they are—as Old Testament prophets— moving at the level of empirical observation and ethical and religious (quite justified) judgment. This is no doubt also present, although in a humanist form, in Marxism. A revolutionary theory, nevertheless, moves at least two steps further: (1) It purports to give a rational, verifiable, and coherent account of the causes, dynamics, and direction of the process and (2) it offers a corresponding rational, calculated, organized, and verifiable strategy for overcoming the present situation.[8] We have already noted that the theory must be constantly checked and corrected. But, quite apart from these corrections, its existence poses theological questions which we dare not evade if we aim to overcome mere good will and irrelevant generosity.

One theological issue which claims our attention in this respect is the question of efficacious love. Two points need to be mentioned briefly. The first is that the commandment of love must evidently be read in the context of Jesus' proclamation of the Kingdom of God. It cannot, therefore, be reduced to a purely interpersonal or intersubjective dimension, but must be set in relation to the eschatological and cosmic scope of the Kingdom. This means that love is inextricably interwoven with hope and justice. The second point follows. Love is not exhausted in the area of intentionality and demonstration but it is other-directed and demands efficacy. It is not content to express and demonstrate, it intends to accomplish. The French theologian Ricoeur has succinctly put it:

> If love is a category of the Kingdom of God and, as such, it implies an eschatological dimension, then it equals justice. We show little or no understanding of love when we make charity the counterpart and supplement of, or the substitute for, justice; love is co-extensive with justice; it is its soul, its impulse, its deep motivation; it lends it its vision, which is the other, the absolute value of which it testifies. . . .At the same time, justice is the efficacious, institutional, and social realization of love.[9]

A second theological issue that needs to be clarified is the background of the concept of peace as it is commonly used and the problem of violence. At the risk of oversimplification, I want to sketch the two theological perspectives which seem to me to find expression in the current discussion of these issues. One of them is built on the principle of the rationality of the universe—the conviction that a universal order penetrates the world. Heaven and earth, nature and society, moral and spiritual life seek the equilibrium that corresponds to their rational place, and the preservation of this order is the supreme value. Whatever perturbs it becomes "a trampling of reason." In its most crass form, this concept simply becomes an ideological screen (to use Ricoeur's expression) to hide the injustice of the status quo by identifying it with cosmic rationality. Violence is understood in the light of this order: whatever disturbs it is irrational and evil and ought to be countered through a rational use of coercion. This logic, undoubtedly plagued with fallacies, nevertheless, flourishes in the "Christian" rhetoric of the right. The will of God coincides with the ordering of things, which in turn coincides with the present order, threatened by "the violent ones." To resist the threat is to obey God.

This is not the place to engage in a detailed analysis of this theological point of view. It can, of course, be formulated in a more guarded way, avoiding a direct identification of the rational order of things with the existing one and positing a normative order—such as the concept of a natural law in its various older and newer forms—which can even justify a certain "subversive violence." Nevertheless, the question remains as to the historical roots of both the idea and the content of such natural law. As to the former, it seems to me possible to trace it to the philosophical rationalization of a mythology of the "cosmos" which in turn sacralizes a static and stratified society. As to the contents of such natural law, it has often been noted that it reproduces some set of historical conditions—whether of the past or of the present. The historically undeniable fact that this theological perspective came to dominate Christianity at the time when this latter was co-opted as the religious undergirding and sanction of the empire is in itself a very significant comment.

The other perspective conceives man as a project of liberation that constantly emerges in the fight against the objectifications given in nature, in history, in society, in religion. Man is a creator, and creation is always, in some measure, a violence exerted on things as they are. It is an affirmation of the new against "that which is"; it is an eruption that can only make room for itself by exploding the existing systems of integration. Violence plays a creative role in this scheme as the "midwife" (even though I don't think that Marx's famous dictum can be totally interpreted in this perspective). This conception can also be escalated to the extreme, elevating violence as an ultimate principle of creation, valid in itself because it is, par excellence, the destruction of all objectifications. Only in the destruction of everything that limits him—nature, social order, ethical norm, divinity—can man find his freedom, i.e., his humanity. But even without looking for these extreme formulations, it is possible to conceive history as a dialectic in which the negation through which the new can emerge implies always a certain measure of violence.

As theological positions, both perspectives find support in the biblical and ecclesiastical tradition. They are frequently identified respectively with the priestly and prophetic streams and it would not be difficult to trace both currents in the history of Christian theology. They have given rise to two different understandings of peace which deserve mention in connection with our subject. The first one equates peace with order, lack of conflict, harmonious integration—one would almost say "ecological balance in nature and society." The German theologian Hans P. Schmidt[10] finds its roots in the Babylonian myth of society as a living organism and thinks that it finds expression in the wisdom tradition in the Bible. It dominates the Greco-Roman conception of peace and has shaped the theological tradition since Augustine. The other view of peace is typically represented by the phophets but can be shown, I think, to be the predominant one in the Bible. Peace is a dynamic process through which justice is established amid the tensions of history. The Catholic Latin American Conference of bishops at Medellín (1968)[11] has summarized well this view of peace as a work of justice, an ever renewed task, and a fruit of active love. It is quite evident that the possibility of conflict will be differently viewed in these two conceptions. For the first it will be in itself negative, a rupture in harmony; for the second it may be a positive manifestation of the situation which requires righting. Violence in the more specific sense of physical compulsion or destruction may be accepted or rejected in either of the two views, but acceptance or rejection will be viewed in a different way. In the first it will be judged in terms of order; in the second, in terms of the struggle for justice.

Recent discussions tend to be polarized along these two theological traditions. While I think that they represent significant dimensions of Christian thought, I want to suggest that their approach is seriously distorted and needs correction. In making order and rationality on the one hand or freedom and conflict on the other the basic starting points for theological reflection, they miss, I think, the biblical starting point, which is never an abstract notion or principle, but a concrete situation. The Bible does not conceive man and society as a function of reason or freedom but in concrete historical relations of man-things-God. Even if we try to understand the basic biblical notions of justice, mercy, faithfulness, truth, peace, we are always thrown back to concrete stories, laws, invitations, commandments; they are defined as an announced action or commandment of God in a given historical situation. This does not mean, to be sure, that these words are empty sounds covering a number of capricious and heterogeneous events but it does mean that ethical criteria are not defined a-temporally but in relation to the concrete conditions of existence of men historically located. These facts taken together do represent a direction—the Kingdom of God—in terms of which one may speak of worthy or unworthy actions. But this direction cannot be translated into a universal principle—reason, order, liberty, conflict.

Against this background, violence appears in the Bible, not as a general form of human conduct which has to be accepted or rejected as such, but as an element of God's announcement-commandment, as concrete acts which must be carried out or avoided in view of a result, of a relation, of a project indicated by the announcement-commandment. Thus, the law forbids certain forms of violence to persons and things and authorizes and even commands others. There are wars that are commanded—even against Israel—and wars that are forbidden—even on behalf of Israel. If one tries to find some coherence in these indications, a first and simple formulation might be that the invitation to exercise or renounce conflict and violence

117

tends to open the space in which men (concretely as foreigner, widow, orphan, poor, family) can be and do, on earth, that which belongs to their particular humanity. In general, it seems possible to say that conflict and violence are means to break out of conditions (slavery, venegance, arbitrariness, oppression, lack of protection, usurpation) that leave a man, a group of people, or a people unable to be and act as a responsible agent ("as a partner in the covenant") in relation to the others, to things, to God. If this is so, it will not be surprising that, in general terms, peace is preferable to hostility, generosity to vindictiveness, production to destruction, trust and harmony to threat and fear. At this point, the idea of order and rationality has its significant place in Christian reflection. But, given the conditions in which—according to Scripture—human life develops, it is also not surprising that God's announcement-commandment comes almost always as a call to the creation of a new situation, to a transformation and righting of the status quo. This is the priority to which the insistence on liberation legitimately points. Nevertheless, liberation and order, conflict and integration are not conceptual keys for a philosophy of history but heuristic elements for a reflection on God's Word in a given historical situation. They are not, moreover, symmetrical elements; the biblical perspective, centered in the person and work of Jesus Christ, always incorporates order, rationality, preservation in a dynamics of transformation and not the reverse.

If we try to bring together the two theological themes developed in the last pages—efficacious love and the conditions of peace and conflict—in order to return to our specific problem of class struggle, we can say that this question cannot be debated abstractly, but in relation to God's announcement-commandment in Jesus Christ of a new man and a new humanity which must be witnessed to and proleptically anticipated in history. We shall return in the next chapter to the relation between the eschatological expectation and the historical realization. Now we must try to make a few points, in the light of our theological understanding, concerning the concrete problem of the Christian in the class struggle.

Class struggle is a fact. This is not Marx's discovery. Even Calvin, with keen realism, describes the economic and social realms, under the sway of sin, as a battlefield in which greed and self-seeking have destroyed an original community of justice and introduced exploitation, injustice, and disorder.[12] When a fact is introduced in Christian reflection, one cannot be satisfied with merely recording it; it demands to be understood both in its operation and significance and to be theologically evaluated. At this point the Marxist analysis is, I think, indispensable. It must be corrected and refined in the context of action and theory, but it is, so far, the best instrument we have to understand the fact. It teaches us to see class struggle, not as a general consequence of sin, nor as a deplorable accident, but—as Calvin himself saw—as a war prompted by greed and power. More specifically, in our Western capitalist society, it is an effort of the dominating class to protect and maintain the present economic system beyond the time of its ability to provide for the basic needs of all mankind and to organize the productive forces of man and his technological discoveries in such a way that all men may realize their creative potentialities. Class struggle is, finally, the effort of the oppressed to break into a new form of economic and social organization in which work will be related to need and creation and not to profit. It is a struggle for the power to reshape society. It is not a mere outlet for resentment, or an instrument of revenge—although these things are by no means absent—but a means for attaining a new and more just situation. When the fact of class struggle—in itself a brute fact unleashed by the capitalist organization of work and production—is consciously assumed by the working class and deliberately used for its liberation, it becomes a political act. It is as such that it must be theologically evaluated.

If class struggle is a fact; if its dynamics is what we have broadly sketched, then a love which intends to be effective in terms of God's Kingdom cannot avoid taking sides. Why is it, therefore, that so often Christian ethics and ecclesiastical pronouncements flounder precisely at this point? Why is it that they so stubbornly refuse to come to terms with this reality and choose instead to ignore it and to offer plans and projects that presuppose a harmony and coordination of interests and goals of the classes which do not exist? Why is it that ecclesiastical pronouncements, after recognizing the intolerable injustice of the situation and even singling out the economic and social structures responsible for it, issue an appeal to the beneficiaries of the situation and a condemnation of the struggle of the oppressed to change it? Why is it that they can't see that the end—though involuntary—result of such unreality and such well-meaning advice is an acknowledgment and thus a reinforcement of those very structures and powers recognized as oppressive and unjust, a weakening of the struggle through which change can effectively come about in *history*? What is the source of this strange blindness to the unmistakable lesson of history that no significant human group, empire, or class has voluntarily yielded power, that no changes have taken place except through the pressure of those below or outside? There is no possibility of speaking a meaningful word to the working class and to dependent countries unless the facts underlying this contradiction are unmasked and overcome.

Paul Ricoeur has spoken in this respect of "an ideological screen"[13] which he identifies as "the ideology of conciliation at any price." It claims to be based in the Christian faith and systematically denies positive value to any confrontation. We have already seen the theological roots of this ideology—the sacralizing of order and consequently the rejection of anything that threatens or disturbs the present balance—however precarious or unsatisfactory it may be—as a demonic intrusion. Few things are today as necessary and urgent as the exposure and elimination of this ideological screen. It must clearly be shown that this idea of conciliation has nothing to do with biblical reconciliation, or with the "reconciliation of all things in Christ." Reconciliation means in the Bible not the ignoring or explaining away of the contradiction but its effective removal. Jew and Gentile are not invited to minimize or sidestep their difference but to become aware that the contradiction between them had objectively been eliminated through the struggle and sacrifice of Jesus. The differences of man and woman, slave and lord, Greek and Jew are not conciliated in the new fellowship but are overcome through repentance and conversion and the creation of a new man. The "new age" does not coexist pacifically with the "old age" but engages in a death struggle. Reconciliation is not achieved by some sort of compromise between the new and the old but through the defeat of the old and the victory of the new age. The ideological appropriation of the Christian doctrine of reconciliation by the liberal capitalist system in order to conceal the brutal fact of class and imperialist exploitation and conflict is one—if not *the* — major heresy of our time. The explanation for its almost uncontested predominance is no doubt to be found in the insertion of ecclesiastical and theological structures in the oppressive class, in the consequent exclusion of the oppressed as agents of ecclesiastical leadership and theological reflection, in the hold of the system on the mind and interests of the churches. Significantly, this ideology begins to be challenged as a "Church of the oppressed" emerges and begins to find a voice.

The quotations at the beginning of this chapter still demand an answer. Is not struggle, and particularly violence, after all is said, incompatible with Christ's clear example and command of universal love and nonresistance? We can't take this question lightly. But neither can we tolerate its ideological manipulation. In fact, it is an important element for a rethinking of the Christ image which is very important. First of all, we must point out that the Gospels do not admit an interpretation of Jesus' love for all men as tolerance, compromise, or acceptance of evil or as good-natured, easygoing bonhomie. Did he not love the scribes and pharisees whom he violently and consistently criticized and condemned? Did he not love Herod to whom he referred with contempt as "that fox"? Do we not read that he loved the rich young ruler whom he sent away after requesting an absolute renouncement of the riches to which he clung? The examples can be multiplied. Either Jesus excluded from his love a very significant number and, what is more important, whole groups of people, or love must be interpreted in such a way that it may include condemnation, criticism, resistance, and rejection. Within the total biblical view, and in connection with the Kingdom, I think that love must be so reinterpreted. In this sense, Giulio Girardi's words are a good summary:

> Undoubtedly the gospel commands us to love the enemy, but it does not say that we should not have enemies or that we must not combat them. It could not say it; we could not love them concretely without having them. By commanding us to abandon neutrality, the gospel forces us to create enemies and to combat them. . . . The Christian must love everybody, but not all in the same way: we love the oppressed defending and liberating him; the oppressor, accusing and combating him. Love compels us to fight for the liberation of all those who live under a condition of objective sin. The liberation of the rich and the liberation of the poor are realized at the same time. In this way, paradoxically, class struggle not only does not contradict the universality of love but becomes demanded by it.[14]

Frequently we are reminded, when making this point, that Jesus did not identify himself with the struggle of the Zealots of his time for the liberation of his country. The gospel data for this question is, as we know, the object of a complex and heated debate among specialists. Without prejudging the result of this discussion, we must note one thing. If, for whatever reason, Jesus did not enroll himself with the Zealots (and this seems beyond doubt), he did not seem to have left any doubts about whether he was on the side of the poor and oppressed or the power structures (religious and political) of his time. When the crucial moment arrived, he was judged and executed as a subversive. If a Christian wants to follow in his steps and make his option for nonviolence credible, he will have to make sure that he has so clearly made his choices that he will unequivocally be convicted for the subversion of the oppressive order! One may doubt that this is the case in much that poses as *Christian* rejection of violence. To point out that this was simply "a miscarriage of justice" is a very superficial interpretation.[15] The condemnation of Jesus as subversive was not a wrong judgment; it was a wrong understanding of a real fact. He was rightly (from the point of view of the power structure) accused of having taken the side of the oppressed against the constituted religious and political authorities. He was wrongly convicted of having assumed the role of religio-political leader in an armed conspiracy. Unless we take both facts with utmost seriousness we are apt to void Christ's death of historical significance.

The fact remains, nevertheless, that Jesus rejected the role of messianic leader of an armed revolt and chose the way of the cross. This is no mere accident but is deeply rooted in his self-understanding as God's suffering servant. Moreover, he points his community to the same road: they are called to renounce self-defense and the struggle for power and to offer themselves, with the oppressed and on behalf of all, as signs of God's incoming new age of liberation and justice. What is the meaning of this? I think that the clue must be sought in Jesus' temptations (which Matthew and Luke summarize at the beginning of his ministry) in which the political question is clearly in the forefront. What he rejected there was not the political realm but an interpretation of the messianic role in terms of political power. God's anointed is not sent to assume human political struggle in the realm of divine omnipotence but to identify himself with the impotence of the oppressed. Renouncing power meant for him renouncing the exercise of divine power to settle men's affairs ("Who has placed me among you as judge or a divider of property?"). He could only witness to this total humanization of God's participation in man's liberation by the surrender of the cross. In doing this, Jesus did introduce a distance between the old and the new dispensation. The difference does not reside in a privatization or spiritualization of religion but in a secularization of politics. In his incarnation in Jesus Christ God makes room for man to conduct his affairs, to create his history. He will not claim a location on earth and history from which he will bring divine power to bear on human struggles. His location in human history is a proclamation of his Kingdom and an invitation.

For the Christian community this means, as I see it, at least two things. On the one hand, there is no divine war, there is no specifically *Christian* struggle. Christians assume, and participate in, human struggles by identifying with the oppressed. But they have no particularly divine or religious power to contribute. There is no room for crusades, for sacred wars. Secondly, it means that Christians are called to use for this struggle the same rational tools that are at the disposal of all human beings. There is no short-cutting of analysis, ideology, strategy, tactics. There is no divine substitute for the painful and long processes of history. This truism deserves to be mentioned, for Christians have frequently confused human analysis, strategy, and tactics (usually the one that their class or nation had adopted) as the *Christian* way, refusing to test it in historical and rational terms. This is certainly the case in the preference for conciliation, development, and reformism over against revolution and class struggle to which we have referred.

In a story of the Chilean writer Andrés Sabella, the Virgin Mary, aching for the injustice and the suffering on the earth, asks the Son for a miracle. He answers: "Mother, heaven (in Spanish the same word as "sky") will be red until men will simply be men, without poor and rich. There is nothing we can do. Nevertheless, we will give those who fight for it the help of

124

lightning and fire. . . ."[16] Less poetically, the Dutch theologian serving in Argentina, Lambert Schuurman, puts it in this way:

> . . . we cannot delegate this responsibility [planning for the world] to someone else since we take seriously man as partner and cooperator with God. I am convinced of the need for man to work, to make history and not to lose time in creating partial or total sacralizations of reality. . . .On this point there can be no controversy with Marxists: the world and its future are our business and we cannot delegate it to anyone else. . . .We have already noted . . . that it is in no way permitted to speak, in this context, of God's absence. In this sense he *wants* to be absent in order to give to his partner the space needed to fulfill his work.[17]

We must return briefly to the question of the use of violence in the service of the revolution. Marx's and Engels's polemics against the utopian socialism of men like Proudhon or Dühring contend that the violence of the existing system is inevitable because of the conditions of production of the capitalist system; revolutionary violence is necessary because there is no other way of overturning that system. "Violence is the midwife of all old societies pregnant with new ones," indicates the *Communist Manifesto*. Lenin extends this interpretation: "The substitution of the proletarian for the bourgeois state is impossible without a violent revolution."[18] This violence is instrumental and introduces the conditions that will eliminate violence. The state—according to Marxism—is "violence organized"; consequently only the extinction of the state (which does not mean the elimination of organization and administration) that socialism preludes and the classless society to which it will lead will mean "the destruction . . . of all organized and systemic violence, of all violence against men in general . . . " (Lenin).[19] The need for violent revolution is for Marxism neither a principle nor a dogma; it is a hypothesis drawn from history and revolutionary praxis. As such it is open to correction, not merely on theoretical or ethical grounds but only through the historical realization of a true transistion to socialism by nonviolent means. This has been tried in several Latin American countries (Chile, Peru, possibly Argentina), but it is still too soon to draw clear consequences one way or the other from these experiences. There has not yet been any basic change and, on the other hand, the brutal facts of the military coup in Chile in 1973 place a severe restriction on any optimism in this respect.

I have tried to sketch in this concrete, even pragmatic way the background for some remarks on the use of revolutionary violence, because it is only thus that the real nature of the issue can be properly visualized. To approach it from a theoretical discussion would seem to presuppose that we are living in a neutral situation in which we are called to decide whether we shall use violence or not. The point scarcely needs to be made that in a continent where thousands perish daily, victims of diverse forms of violence, such a neutral situation does not exist. *My* violence is direct or indirect, institutional or insurrectional, conscious or unconscious. But it is violence; it objectively produces victims, whether I intend it subjectively or not. Even a staunch opponent of the use of insurrectional violence like Archbishop Dom Helder Cámara states his case in these terms:

[armed revolt] is legitimate but impossible. Legitimate because it is provoked and impossible because it would be squashed. . . .My position in this regard is not based on religious motives, but on tactical ones. It isn't based on any idealism, but on a realistic, purely political sense. . . .I detest any one who remains unperturbed, or silent, and I love only those who fight, who dare to do something.[20]

A significant discussion of this issue can therefore be only a discussion on the *violences* and the conditions of violence in our concrete situation. It has to do with who inflicts these different violences and who suffers from them, with the purposes of these different violences, and how these purposes are accomplished (or not) through their use. We must resist all hypostatization of *la violencia,* either to defend it or to attack it. The discussion of

violence can only be adjectival of the entire process in movement in Latin America and of the struggle for liberation. Such
sentences as "we are against violence, wherever it may come
from" or "we reject all forms of violence" may be quite "seduc-
tive for human and Christian sensibility,"[21] as Girardi says but,
as he himself goes on to say, they are only hypocritical self-
justification or unconscious cooperation with existing oppressive violence. They can only make sense on the lips of people—
who do not usually employ them—who are actively and dan-
gerously involved in the removal of prevalent violence.

Nonviolent action is not only most appropriate to the Christian conscience but also to the revolutionary purpose. As Lenin
points out in the quotation previously mentioned, the goal of
revolution is the removal of violence. Insofar as nonviolent
action respects the human person, makes room for an internalization of the project of liberation in the masses and fosters the
sense of solidarity in the construction of a new society, it is the
means most coherent with the revolutionary purpose. Moreover, when efficacy (which, as we saw, cannot be separated
from Christian love) does require the use of violence for overturning an oppressive system, it creates a number of very serious problems: the exacerbation of hate, resentment, and rival-
ries, the imposition of changes from a structure of power
without a corresponding development of conscience, the acceptance of "the rules of the game" of the present oppressive
system. Victorious revolutionary violence runs the risk of simply substituting one form of oppression for another and thus
becoming really counterrevolutionary. It certainly makes the
construction (human, economic, social, institutional, political)
necessary after the takeover of power all the more difficult,
almost in proportion to the amount and the length of the period
of subversive violence.

Precisely this same consideration of the human cost of revolution and the health of the ensuing process which leads us to
reject absolute violence is the one which prevents us from

embracing absolute pacifism. Nonviolence has also to ask what is the human cost in lives, suffering, paralyzing frustration, dehumanization, and the introjection of a slave-consciousness. We pay for our choice of means for change. No sentimentalism can replace the sober assessment of the situation. A Christian ethics cannot take refuge in the subjective appeal to "my conscience" or satisfy itself with a readiness to suffer violence without resistance. For it is not our life or comfort as Christians which is at stake—at this point the Christian community can only follow the road of the cross—but the life and humanity of our neighbor. Certainly Christians in the struggle for liberation will witness to their faith—as well as to the ultimate goal of the revolution—by insisting on counting carefully the cost of violence, by fighting against all idolization of destruction and the destructive spirit of hate and revenge, by attempting to humanize the struggle, by keeping in mind that beyond victory there must be reconciliation and construction. But they cannot block through Christian scruples the road clearly indicated by a lucid assessment of the situation. Even less can they play the game of reaction lending support to those who are profiting from present violence or weakening through sentimental pseudo-Christian slogans (however well-meaning) the will among the oppressed to fight for their liberation.

The Russian Orthodox philosopher Nicolas Berdyaev called our attention more than forty years ago to the fact that Marxism was "a secularized eschatology": "He [Marx] confessed in a secularized form, i.e., loosed from its religious roots, the old Jewish messianism."[22] This becomes most clear in relation to the problem of the existence of classes, their conflict, and violence. Revolution, the dictatorship of the proletariat, the establishment of socialism, the progressive extinction of the state, the transition to communism, are the stages through which classes disappear into a classless society, social conflict is replaced by solidarity, and violence becomes extinct because its

128

causes have been removed. It is only then that real history, the realm of freedom, begins for humanity.

A very popular *Handbook of Marxism-Leninism,* published by Kuusinen in the U.S.S.R., uses for the description of this final phase of communism expressions such as these: "Communism is the society that puts a final stop to need and misery"; "human work is entirely liberated of all that . . . made of it a heavy load"; "[communism] is a classless society in which the last remnants of inequality and social differences are eliminated"; "it brings with it the final triumph of human freedom" because "it creates the conditions in which coercion becomes absolutely unnecessary"; "the relations of imposition and hierarchy are definitively replaced by free cooperation"; the conditions are created "for an unlimited development of personality and the physical and spiritual fulfillment of man"; "the participation in the direction of society will become an intense activity for all citizens, as intimately felt and as customary as participation in socially valuable work"; "communist man will not be egoist or individualist"; war will have no room in such a society: on the contrary, "communism will inspire a new and higher meaning to the very concept of humanity by making of the human race . . . a single universal community." And all of this, far from being a static goal, is an endless march toward "glittering peaks of civilization" and human development which we can still not even surmise.[23]

It is possible to smile cynically at these predictions, and to point out that socialist societies do not show signs of moving very rapidly in this direction. Cynicism in the face of man's aspiration for total redemption is hardly appropriate for Christians. Besides, one cannot but note the profound analogy between some of these predictions and prophetic descriptions of the Day of the Lord . . . which so far have also not been fulfilled. Revolution and the Christian faith equally look forward to a final reconciliation of all things. But they see differently the relation of the present struggle, achievements, and progress to this final consummation. This difference, in turn, ought to be reflected in the way in which we act in the midst of historical conflicts. If this is so, the difference between the two is not that Christianity teaches reconciliation while revolution incites to conflict (we have seen that Christian love does not exclude conflict nor revolutionary struggle renounce reconciliation). Rather, it consists in the fact that, in their common engagement in the creation of a new society, Christian and non-Christian revolutionaries relate in a different way their immediate revolutionary goal and their final hope. "As a Marxist Christian," said a friend of mine recently at a joint meeting, "I believe in the socialist revolution. As a Christian Marxist, I believe in the Second Coming of Jesus Christ." What difference does this make? It is in this direction that we must continue our exploration.

NOTES

[1] Guillermo Blanco, *El Evangelio según Judas* (Santiago, Chile: Pineda Libros, 1972), p. 86.

[2] *Cristianos por el socialismo,* p. 188. I have tried to analyze the questions arising from the discussion between the Cardinal and the organizers of the debate in "¿Partidismo o solidaridad?" *Cristianos por el socialismo: Exigencias de una opción,* pp. 103-110.

[3] "Documento Final," part I, 1.4; 1.12-18; part II, 1.2-7, 9, 10.

[4] Sergio Arce, in *Religion in Cuba,* ed. A. Hageman and Ph. Wheaton (New York: Association Press, 1971), p. 230.

[5] Gutiérrez, *A Theology of Liberation,* chap. XIII.

[6] Ibid., p. 301 (the translation is ours).

[7] Karl Barth, *Church Dogmatics* (Edinburgh: T. & T. Clark), vol. II/1, p. 386.

[8] This is the emphasis that we find in the documents of "Christians for socialism"; cf. *supra,* Chapter Three.

[9] Paul Ricoeur, "El conflicto ¿signo de contradicción y de unidad?", *Criterio* (Buenos Aires: May 24, 1973), no. 1668, p. 255.

[10] Hans P. Schmidt, "Schalom: Die hebraisch-christliche Provokation," in *Weltfrieden und Revolution,* ed. Hans Eckehard Bahr (Rohwolt: Kreuz Verlag, 1968), pp. 185-235.

[11] The document "On Peace," in *Between Honesty and Hope,* pp. 201 ff., esp. par. 14 (p. 205).

[12] Cf. André Bieler, *La Pensée économique et sociale de Calvin* (Geneva: Librairie de l'Université, 1959), *passim*. Also, by the same author, *L'Humanisme social de Calvin* (Geneva; Labor et Fides, 1961).

[13] Ricoeur, "El conflicto," pp. 253-254.

[14] Giulio Girardi, *Amor cristiano y lucha de clases* (Salamanca; Ediciones Sígueme, 1971), p. 57.

[15] Jürgen Moltmann, *The Crucified God* (New York: Harper & Row, 1974), pp. 131 ff.

[16] Andres Sabella, *Célula Cristo* (Santiago, Chile: Pineda Libros, 1972), p. 25.

[17] Lamberto Schuurman, *El cristiano, la iglesia y la revolución* (Buenos Aires: La Aurora, 1970), pp. 118-119.

[18] Lenin, "El estado y la revolución," *Obras escogidas* (Buenos Aires: Editorial Sudamericana, 1968), vol. III, p. 214.

[19] Ibid., p. 217.

[20] In the interview mentioned above, see Chapter Three, n. 9.

[21] Girardi, *Amor cristiano . . .*, pp. 68-69.

[22] Nicolas Berdyaev, *El cristianismo y el problema del comunismo* (Buenos Aires: Espasa-Calpe, 1944), p. 30

[23] Otto V. Kuusinen, *Manual de marxismo-leninismo* (Buenos Aires: Editorial Fundamentos, 1964), pp. 689 ff.

Chapter Seven

Kingdom of God, Utopia, and Historical Engagement

The relation between Christian eschatology and the Marxist vision of the future has been pointed out often enough. It is interesting to note that for Engels—who devoted quite a bit of attention to the origins and development of the Christian religion—there was an even more important similarity between early Christianity and the socialist movement. "The history of early Christianity," he writes, "has notable points of resemblance with the modern working-class movement."[1] He summarizes it in four points: both are originally a movement of oppressed people; both "preach forthcoming salvation from bondage and misery"; both are persecuted, discriminated, and despised, and both "forge victoriously, irresistibly ahead." He goes so far as to say that Christianity was the form in which socialism was possible and even became dominant within the historical possibilities of the first centuries. The unavoidably religious form that the rebellion of the oppressed took at that time meant that the hope for liberation was projected to another, heavenly world. In that sense, like all religious movements, it falls under the well-known Marxist criticism of being an imaginary substitute for real liberation. On the other hand, lacking the scientific instruments of analysis, its aspirations share the imaginary and fantastic features of utopian socialism.

There is no doubt that the ardent expectation of the total

transformation of the world and the advent of the Kingdom of God was soon replaced in Christianity by a spiritualized and individualistic hope for immortal, celestial life. Whether and to what extent this transformation was due to the influence of the Hellenistic culture, to the delay of the *Parousia,* to the influence of the mystery religions, to the sociologically necessary phenomenon of the institutionalization of the *ecclesia* is for us at this point a question which can remain unanswered. What matters most is to realize the importance of the conception of two worlds: this present, temporal, earthly one, which had a preparatory, contingent, and even at points negligible value, and the eternal one which is the true realm of life, fulfillment and happiness, the goal for the Christian.

The connection between these two worlds came to be seen almost exclusively in terms of the moral and religious life of the individual. Temporal, collective life has no lasting significance except as it may help or hinder the individual to achieve and/or to express the religious and moral virtues which belong to the Christian life. The hope of the Kingdom, far from awakening an ethos to transform the world in the direction of that which was expected, worked as a deterrent for historical action. The Christian and the Marxist utopias (to use this equivocal word) had, therefore, quite opposite historical consequences. The latter galvanizes for action, the former leads to accommodation to present conditions; the latter lends value and meaning to history, the former empties history of meaning and value; the latter legitimizes immediate and provisory stages and achievements, the former relativizes them and makes differences among them irrelevant. Are these consequences intrinsic to the Christian gospel? If not, how can they be overcome, both theologically and practically? This is the issue that we have to explore.

The consideration of this question seems to me to involve at least three issues: the problems of the "two worlds" or, as we shall see, of the "two histories"; the possibility of an intrinsic, substantial—and not merely formal—connection between historical action and eschatological expectation, and the determination of the necessary historical mediations. We shall try in the remainder of this chapter to suggest an initial approach to these issues.

There is scarcely a question of "two histories" in relation to the Old Testament. There, God's action takes place in history and as history. It inextricably involves human action and, conversely, there is no human action reported outside the relation with God's purpose and word. This interconnection does not mean an equation between God's sovereignty and history, as if the former would justify or sacralize everything that happens— as in the rationalist optimism of Voltaire's Pangloss, or as if history would unambiguously fulfill God's will. But the distinction is conceived *polemically:* the lordship of Yahweh is an efficacious word which becomes history and creates history by convoking and rejecting men and peoples in relation to God's purpose. Thus, Yahweh's sovereignty does not appear in history as an abstract act or an interpretation but as announcement and commandment, as an announcement which convokes, as promise and judgment demanding and inviting a response. History is, precisely, this conflict between God and his people in the midst and in relation to all peoples.

Two more points must be emphasized in this connection. The first is that any separation between the brute facts of history and their prophetic interpretation is alien to the Bible and originates in the Greek epistemological split between brute facts and *logos.* The prophetic message is for the Old Testament an act and a factor in itself. It is not primarily destined to explain but to call, to invite, to condemn. I think it is possible to show that the liturgical and the didactic word belong in this same category. Secondly, we must stress the *political* character of this history, i.e., as action and word embracing the total life of the people and of peoples as collective entities and the reality of power. Every attempt to separate the political from the religious areas in the Old Testament is completely artificial. Even the more personal manifestations—like Moses' or Isaiah's vocation, the moving episode of Ruth and Naomi, the prayers of the Psalms—are indissolubly worked into this movement of the peoples and "God's people." God polemicizes with the peoples and through them. The covenant is sealed within this conflict. In the kings and judges, laws and worship, commerce and art, internal life and external relations of this people, Yahweh conflictively asserts his sovereignty by calling and rejecting, forgiving and punishing, and thus erecting the signs and the road of his coming final victory, his Kingdom.

Nobody can fail to see that we move into a somewhat different climate as we enter the New Testament, particularly the Pauline and Johannine literature. The question is to determine what is the difference. Some of the traditional explanations of this change seem to originate in Greek intellectualism and smack of Gnostic and Marcionite heresy. These are the explanations that claim that the New Testament is more spiritual or religious than the Old. We remain in the same area of ideas when the "individualism" of the New Testament is placed over against the "collectivism" of the Old. Modern theological research has amply refuted the basis for these interpretations—although, curiously enough, many times returning to them in other forms!

It is not enough, nevertheless, to reject false explanations. Where does, in fact, the difference in "climate" lie between the expectation of God's Kingdom and the movement of history in the Old and the New Testaments? I advance the following thesis. In the New Testament, the history of salvation acquires a certain "density" of its own, a certain "distance" in relation to the totality of human history. It is not—let us be clear about it—that we have now a separate history: it is still the story of Herod, of Pilate, or of the merchants of Ephesus. But as a new mission emerges, which is indissolubly tied to a particular historical nucleus (the history of Israel and of Jesus Christ), which becomes dated in time, the faith of the converted "heathen" becomes related to a twofold historical reference: their own history and this other one, which now comes to be constitutive for their faith. In other words, while the salvific memory or recollection of Israel was one with their historical memory as a people, with their historical project, the memory of the converted Gentile, without losing its connection with the latter, incorporates this other, "alien" history, the story of Israel and of Jesus the Christ. To confess the Kingdom is not for us, Gentile Christians, only to enter into the heritage of our own history but at the same time to take distance from it and to become engrafted into this other one. It is to confess the exodus, the exile, Bethel and Nazareth, the Golgotha and the tomb of Joseph of Arimathea as our own—and this not merely in their significance or in their exemplariness but in their particular and unrepeatable historicity. Consequently, an inevitable duality of histories appear. We Gentiles, in distinction to Israel, cannot believe without this double historical reference and, therefore, without asking ourselves how to relate God's action to this double historical reference in which the gospel involves us.

With some few and notable exceptions, the line of solution has been dualistic. With due reserve, we can trace it back to Augustine's *City of God*. Essentially, it consists in relating the Kingdom to one of these histories, the history of faith, which thus becomes a univocal, sacred, and distinct line, and in reducing the other history to a general episodic framework devoid of eschatological significance: a mere stage. It may be debated whether Augustine himself identifies the former history—that of the *civitas dei*—with the Church, but this does not matter so much in the present context. The decisive point is that this is the history of the Kingdom—whether it be identified with the hierarchical, the pious, or the orthodox Church.

This dualistic solution suffers from unsolvable difficulties. On the one hand, the continuity Church-Kingdom is untenable in view of the all too evident failures of the Church. How are we to dodge the fact that the history of faith shares quite plainly the characteristics of secular history and proves to be, in many ways, an empirically undistinguishable parcel of it? Here theologians have introduced all the theories about an invisible Church or the different sectarian solutions. But, on the other hand, neither can a total discontinuity between Kingdom and general history be maintained in view of the witness of Scripture and our own experience of God's presence in the world. It is difficult to read the Bible and to go on saying that general history is a mere episode, unrelated to the Kingdom, and without eschatological significance. The question of the salvation of those heathen who had not heard the gospel but had a right attitude was the first way in which the problem was posed. The doctrine of the *descensus ad inferos* and many theological formulae appearing both in Catholicism and in Protestantism (including certain aspects of the doctrine of predestination which became explicit in Barth) are attempts to explore the salvific contents in general history. But what we meet here is no mere speculation (however speculative and even fantastic some theological formulae may be). As a matter of fact, the numerous references in Jesus' own teaching to the "surprises" at the Last Judgment, to an eschatological inversion, even though their immediate reference may be to Israel, pose the problem of the continuity between general history and the Kingdom or, in other words, of the eschatological significance of human action in love.

Theologians of liberation have decidedly rejected the "dualistic" position. As we have seen, they strive to maintain the integrity of "one single God-fulfilled history," as Gutiérrez puts it. "Monist" formulations are not without precedent. Origen's and Irenaeus' theological perspectives—quite different from each other—can be counted in their camp. But it is in recent theology where a systematic attempt has been made to overcome dualism, as in Moltmann and Metz, by stressing the historical significance of the eschatological expectation as critical questioning and, in our theology, the eschatological value of present historical praxis of liberation. God builds his Kingdom from and within human history in its entirety; his action is a constant call and challenge to man. Man's response is realized in the concrete arena of history with its economic, political, ideological options. Faith is not a different history but a dynamic, a motivation, and, in its eschatological horizon, a transforming invitation.

Very few responsible theologians would openly support today a clear dualistic approach. The God of the prophets and of Jesus Christ can hardly be assimilated to a Gnostic or mystic *soter* of a sect concerned with populating his Olympus with a few souls rescued from the stormy sea of history. The biblical account is clearly incompatible with a "religious" reductionism which consigns to the limbo of irrelevance the history of persons and peoples. But we must admit that theoretical and practical problems are not automatically solved by adopting a monistic solution. In order to give to this *one* history a concrete content, one must find a transcription of the gospel which can be seen as effectively operating in general history. In other words, it is necessary "to name the Kingdom" in the language of everyday human history. There is no lack of precedents and possibilities. As we have seen, we speak of "love," "liberation," "the new man" as the signs which allow us to identify the active sovereignty of God in history, the redeeming presence of Jesus Christ, and, consequently, the call and the obedience of faith. This, we contend, is biblically and theologically legitimate. But a serious risk lurks in this option, because, as these terms are historicized in the general history of mankind, they run the risk of being uprooted, of de-historicizing themselves in the particular historical reference of faith. That is, we come to speak of a love, a new man, a liberation in which the reference to the history of Israel, of Jesus Christ, of the Apostles becomes secondary, or merely exemplary, or dispensable. If this happens we have, in Christian terms, vacated any reference to God himself. What God and whose Kingdom are we speaking about? At the extreme of this line, we would conclude by deifying man and history and it would be more honest to call a spade a spade and to avow a total immanentism. This is not, to be sure, the intention of those of us who attempt to overcome dualism. But how can a theological and practical formulation avoid this risk without falling back on dualism? This is an important task for our theologians, which we cannot avoid.

The question which is posed for us is, in simple terms, how to describe the relation between the two historical references of faith without vacating either one. Or, how do we account for the eschatological significance of general human history? Or, again, how do we return to the eschatological Christian faith the historical dynamism which it seems to have lost?

Do historical happenings, i.e., historical human action in its diverse dimensions—political, cultural, economic—have any value in terms of the Kingdom which God prepares and will gloriously establish in the Parousia of the Lord? If there is such a relation, how shall we understand it? And what is its significance for our action? Juan Luis Segundo has called attention to the fact that European theologians like Moltmann and Metz explicate this relationship with words like "anticipation," "sketch," "analogy." "It seems quite significant for me that none of the terms used," says Segundo, "contains semantically any element of *causality*." He adds a comment which deserves to be quoted:

> If Weth had said, for instance, *analogical* "production" or "creation," we could still doubt between two possible meanings: a change of structures *produces* the Kingdom of God but only in analogies which become progressively better without ever ceasing to be analogies; *or* that structures produce only *images*, analogies of the Kingdom. But, when he says that the political engagement of Christians aims *to present an analogical image*, he clearly decides in favor of the second meaning and against any idea of causality.[2]

Segundo goes on to indicate that this choice results in "a marked reticence to relate action on sociopolitical structures and the building of the Kingdom." This, which might be defended as the protection of God's initiative, in fact results in "a sort of . . . equivalence between right and left over against the danger which . . . the Christian community must fight, namely, absolutization."[3] In other words, historical action is not really significant for the Kingdom; at most, it may succeed to project provisory images which remind us of it. These images must not be taken too seriously in order to avoid absolutizing them. The historical significance of the expectation of the Kingdom is preeminently to protect us from any too strong commitment to a present historical project!

In this way, progressive European and American theology tends to reinforce, through a quite different theological route, the dualistic relativizing of historical action. This may seem too summary a judgment. A detailed study would, I think, qualify it but without refuting the main point: any extrinsic relation between Kingdom and history is insufficient to support a serious concrete engagement. But is any other relation biblically justified? We must recognize that the New Testament gives us scanty elements to answer this question. This is due, I believe, to its peculiar historical circumstances. But in the total biblical perspective it seems justified to pose and consider this question in the analogy of the eschatological concepts of "body" and "resurrection."[4] The former concept allows Paul to underline at the same time the continuity and discontinuity between present and risen life, a continuity in which the recognizable identity of the two is asserted together with the transformation of our present historical life. Such a transformation is not a disfiguration or denaturalization of our bodily life but its fulfillment, its perfecting, the elimination of corruptibility and weakness. As a matter of fact, bodily life reaches its true shape, its full meaning—communication, love, praise—in the resurrection. Resurrection, far from being the rescue of a spiritual element in human life, cleansing it from the bodily experience and identity obtained throughout life, is the total redemption of man, the true and unhindered realization of a bodily life cleansed from self-deception and self-seeking (flesh) and made perfect in transparent (glorious) singleness of purpose and experience (spiritual) and full community with God.

Another Pauline concept supplements the previous one: the concept of "works." Once the passion of the polemical age is over, we can again raise the question of the eschatological significance of human works performed in this life. It seems to me that, for Paul, the works fulfilled "in the body," in everyday historical life, have a future to the extent that they belong to the new order, the order of the world of the resurrection, the order of love. They have a future, not because of some merit attributed to them but because they belong to this new order. At the same time, these are works performed within the structures of history, as master or slave, as wife or husband, or son, or authority, or even as a missionary. The decisive Pauline distinction between the works of faith and the works of the law does not refer—it seems to me—to any discrimination between sacred and profane, or merely human and Christian works, but to the relation to the new age, which becomes explicit in love. Since Christ has risen and inaugurated a new realm of life, man's existence in love bears the marks of this new age and will find lasting fulfillment when this new age will become an unresisted and total realization.

For several reasons, into which we cannot enter now, Christian theology and ethics have separated human actions from their historical context and reduced them to their individual significance. Such narrowing seems quite strange to the biblical way of thinking, cast in the conception of eons or ages in which the divine purpose is fulfilled. When we overcome this reductionism it becomes quite normal to assert both continuity and discontinuity between history and the Kingdom of God of the same order as the continuity/discontinuity between earthly

141

body/spiritual body. The Kingdom is not the denial of history but the elimination of its corruptibility, its frustrations, weakness, ambiguity—more deeply, its sin—in order to bring to full realization the true meaning of the communal life of man. In the same vein, historical "works" in all orders of life—social, economic, political—are permanent insofar as they belong to that order. At the same time, all possibilities of confusion are eliminated because, in one case as in the other, there is the intervening fact of judgment which divides, excludes, and cleanses ("burns") that which does not belong in the new age. The Kingdom is not—here we must deepen the meaning of the apocalyptic literature—the natural denouement of history. Quite the contrary, history arrives at the Kingdom through suffering, conflict, and judgment. But the Kingdom redeems, transforms, and perfects the "corporality" of history and the dynamics of love that has operated in it.

If these observations are true, any language which confines the relation between history and the Kingdom to the realm of image-reality remains inadequate. The Kingdom is not merely adumbrated, reflected, foreshadowed, or analogically hinted at in the individual and collective realizations of love in history, but actually present, operative, authentically—however imperfectly and partially—realized. The objections against expressions like "building" the Kingdom are legitimate protests against naïve optimism or at times justified protection of the primacy of divine initiative. But they are usually cast in a quite unbiblical concept of God as a kind of machine programmed to produce certain facts (the incarnation, the Parousia) irrespective of the movement of history. Once we see divine initiative as that action of God within history and in historical terms which opens history toward the promise, we seem not only entitled but required to use the strong language of growth, realization, creation which, furthermore, is that of the prophets and apostles!

When this perspective is adopted, the main question which

recent theology has been asking must also be shifted. Instead of asking, where is the Kingdom present or visible in today's history? we are moved to ask, how can I participate—not only individually but in a community of faith and in a history—in the coming world? The main problem is not noetic but, so to say, empirical. It has to do with an active response. The Kingdom is not an object to be known through adumbrations and signs that must be discovered and interpreted but a call, a convocation, a pressure that impels. History, in relation to the Kingdom, is not a riddle to be solved but a mission to be fulfilled. That mission, one must hasten to add, is not a mere accumulation of unrelated actions, but a new reality, a new life which is communicated in Christ, in the power of the Spirit. How can we participate, act out, *produce* the quality of personal and corporate existence which has a future, which possesses eschatological reality, which concentrates the true history? We face the question of historical mediations for our participation in the building of the Kingdom.

When we ask the question as to how to participate in the Kingdom in our historical action we are, to some extent, thrown back to the tension of the twofold reference of our faith, because the kind of action which corresponds to the Kingdom, has a permanent future, must be one which *names* this future and *corresponds to its quality.* It is therefore impossible to reduce proclamation to the efficacious action of love or vice-versa. Recent ecumenical discussion has frequently been quite agitated on this point. There have been advocates of proclamation and advocates of action. But it seems that much of this discussion is seriously misleading insofar as the two things are seen as either reconcilable through some sort of balance or the one subordinate to the other. Rather, we should see that both action and announcement are eschatologically significant, while their unity is not in our hands. The tension cannot therefore be overcome this side of the full realization of God's Kingdom. Only at that point will all proclamation and all action of

143

love be rescued from their ambiguity, reunited, and perfectly manifested, in the biblical sense of this word. This eschatological unity of that which is named and that which is done is what is intended in the numerous biblical references to the surprising inversions at the Last Judgment. But we live in the tension of this double reference, which is one in Jesus Christ and at the end but never totally one in our experience.

To the extent that this last assertion is true, we have to qualify and correct the emphasis on "one single history." We may even have to ask whether this formulation does not suffer from the still strong influence of the Scholastic view of the relation between nature and grace in which the latter becomes a superstructure built on the basis of the former, with the corresponding danger of mystic absorption of the human into a divine order. Once we take notice of this criticism and accept the tension of the "double historical reference" of our faith, still we have to look at the ethical understanding of this twofold-ness. At this point one of the main divergences between Latin American and European/North American theologians seems to surface. For the latter, it seems, the specific "Christ-reference" relativizes the "present" historical reference of our faith and action. A brief discussion of Moltmann will illustrate the point. The case is most significant because Moltmann is the theologian to whom the theology of liberation is most indebted and with whom it shows the clearest affinity.

In his first and epoch-making book, *Theology of Hope*,[5] the Tübingen theologian convincingly argued that Christian hope, far from leading to easy acceptance of the status quo, is a constant disturbance of reality as it is and a call to move ahead to the future. The God of the promise does not sacralize the present: he opens man for the future and opens a future for man, the future of love, justice, and life which he has promised in the resurrection of Jesus Christ from the dead. This vision was criticized by some theologians as being too optimistic, as conceiving history as a victorious march into the future without recognizing the close relation between resurrection and cross. Others, on the other hand, found Moltmann's description of the "promise" of the hope toward which we move too vague, a tantalizing mirage unable to inspire concrete historical action.[6]

In another major book, *The Crucified God*,[7] Moltmann has brilliantly corrected and deepened his earlier insight, meeting at the same time both criticisms through a concentration on the cross. The tension which we have characterized as the double historical reference of our faith Moltmann defines as a tension between identity and relevance. The relation of the two appears in contemporary Christianity as almost inversely proportional: the greater the involvement in present historical action for the sake of the neighbor, the greater the risk of losing the specific Christian identity; the stronger the consciousness of attachment to the specifically Christian heritage the stronger the risk of isolation from the present struggles of mankind—and therefore of irrelevance. Quite naturally, Moltmann is not satisfied with this situation and looks for an identity which will itself move to relevance and a relevance that will be rooted in identity. This fulcrum he finds in the cross, which is at the same time the test of Christian identity and the point of God's maximum—indeed total and irreversible—commitment to mankind.

God in Christ identifies himself utterly with man oppressed, destituted, and abandoned. He dies the death of the blasphemer, the subversive, the God-forgotten man. His cross marks therefore the bankruptcy of political and religious power, indeed of God conceived as a protective assurance against destitution and death. Here we meet the powerless, suffering, Godforsaken man as the last reality of God himself. Therefore all false optimism, all utopian hope is definitively shattered. But at the same time, we are called to this same identity in the double identification with the crucified Christ, and therefore with those with whom he himself was identified:

the outcast, the oppressed, the poor, the forsaken, the sinners, the lost. This is the cradle of the Christian's identity and relevance. To be crucified together with Christ means to stand with those for whose sake God himself died the death of the sacrilege, the subversive, the Godforsaken one.

Moltmann intends to become very concrete in the historical description of this identification.[8] He names five "demonic circles of death" under which man suffers: poverty, violence, racial and cultural deprivation, industrial destruction of nature, and meaninglessness or Godforsakenness. Consequently, justice, democracy, cultural identity, peace with nature, and meaningful life are the concrete contents of historical hope. Quite clearly this brings us to the area of politics. At this point, Moltmann sees a "political theology of the cross" in opposition to the classical political theologies which glorified and sacralized power. Its function is "to liberate the state from political idolatry and men from political alienation and powerlessness."[9] This "critical function" of de-sacralization and de-ideologization is the "political" task of the Church which finds her identity in the crucifixion and resurrection of Jesus.

Moltmann indicates, at the beginning of the chapter in which he deals with "the political liberation of man," that he writes at this point in dialogue with the theology of liberation as developed in Latin America. His coherent and brilliant argument seems, nevertheless, to fail to grasp the basic challenge of Latin American theological thought and to remain, therefore, within the circle of European political theology. This does not, certainly, minimize the value of his most significant work. We must, nevertheless, try to sharpen the criticism in order to carry forward our dialogue.

Moltmann rightly criticizes the theologies that separate the political and theological realms—which find no relation between God's eschatological order and man's political action in history—and those which find only "analogical," formal relations between the two. He finds inadequate the "idealist" attempt to work out a general perspective and to ask afterward "for concrete realizations of the abstract." "History," he indicates, "is the sacrament of Christian ethics, not only its material."[10] Therefore, we will find God's action *in* the concrete and the historical. But, if this is so, should we not also recognize that it is impossible to reflect on a political theology of the cross without resorting to a historical and concrete way of understanding that "sacrament"? Can we remain satisfied with a general description of "the demonic circles of death," without trying to understand them in their unity, their roots, their dynamics, i.e., without giving a coherent socio-analytical account of this manifold oppression? Are we not taking lightly the stark historical reality of the cross when we satisfy ourselves with an impressionistic description of man's alienation and misery? In other words, it seems that, if theology means to take history seriously, it must incorporate—with all necessary *caveats*—a coherent and all-embracing method of sociopolitical analysis. Moltmann does not seem to be conscious of this need.

One of the consequences of the failure we have indicated is seen in a number of statements which hover between theological normative assertions and historical statements of fact. What is, for instance, the nature of statements such as these: "Christianity was not originated as a national religion and *therefore it cannot become one*,"[11] or: "It *is* not possible to abuse the Christian faith in order to justify a political situation . . ."[12]? In view of other equally strong formulations ("since Constantine . . . Christianity took up the role of the political religion of society . . ."),[13] it is clear that the earlier sentences cannot be taken as naïve assertions of fact. But is it simply possible to put the two things side by side without attempting to account for the relationships? In other words, are we not forced to indicate how was the Christian faith co-opted into a political project, what were the relations to the dominant ideologies, what is the historical dynamics of this process, how is the critical awareness concerning the inadequacy of this synthesis related to historical—socioeconomic, political, ideological—changes? It seems that a point has been reached at which theologians cannot continue to make theological assertions concerning the political and social significance of the gospel without facing the facts of the actual empirical significance of the Christian churches and relating the two things in order that their statements may become *historically* significant and not simply idealistic assertions.

This, in turn, seems to lead to a more serious problem: the failure to give a concrete content to the "identification with the oppressed." Two sentences from this chapter will illustrate the point: "The crucified God is really a God without country and without class. But he is not an a-political God; he is the God of the poor, of the oppressed, of the humiliated."[14] But the poor, the oppressed, the humiliated *are a class* and *live in countries.* Is it really theologically responsible to leave these two sentences hanging without trying to work out their relation? Are we really for the poor and oppressed if we fail to see them as a class, as members of oppressed societies? If we fail to say *how,* are we "for them" in their concrete historical situation? Can we claim a solidarity which has nothing to say about the actual historical forms in which their struggle to overcome oppression is carried forward? It is perhaps necessary to say that "a modern political theology does not intend to dissolve the Church into a politics of right or left."[15] But is it possible to claim a solidarity with the poor and to hover above right and left as if that choice did not have anything to do with the matter?

Moltmann has spoken admirably about God's Kingdom in history:

> The question of liberation is, precisely, not something fixed but in process and can be grasped only by means of a dialectical, engaged thought. . . . The conception of reality as a *sacrament* corresponds to the symbol in thought. . . . These realities are not a realm distinct and separated from God, neither are they mere parables and simili-

tudes of his reign. They are, to take up Luther's expression, synechdocally, real presences of his coming universal presence. In this sense, no theology of liberation, unless it wills to remain within idealism, can do without the materializations of God's presence.[16]

Why is it, therefore, that at the crucial point, Moltmann—and most European theology—draws back from these "materializations" and finds refuge in a "critical function" which is able to remain above right and left, ideologically neutral, independent of a structural analysis of reality? We are told that this is the only way to avoid sacralizing a particular ideology or power structure. I think this is a crucial point, to which we must respond in two ways. On the one hand, it is indeed necessary to reject as strongly as possible any sacralization of ideology and system. In this respect, even such expressions as "materializations of God's presence" or "sacrament" seem to me to run the risk of mystical identifications; there must be no room for theocratic dreams of any sort either from right or from left. But it is important to stress that such a secularization of politics is to be attained not through a new idealism of Christian theology, but through a clear and coherent recognition of historical, analytical, and ideological mediations. There is no *divine* politics or economics. But this means that we must resolutely use the best *human* politics and economics at our disposal.

This brings us to the final point in the discussion. In order to carry through the process of de-sacralizing, of a true secularization of politics, we believe that the European theologians must de-sacralize their conception of "critical freedom" and recognize the human, ideological contents that it carries. When they conceive critical freedom as the form in which God's eschatological Kingdom impinges on the political realm, they are simply opting for *one* particular ideology, that of liberalism. This follows very clearly, for instance, from Metz's description of the process of freedom in the modern world, or from Moltmann's own sketch of "the liberations" (he himself stresses the plural) from the demonic circles. What emerges is one form of the liberal social-democratic project which progressive European theologians seem to cherish particularly. They may be totally justified in this choice. The only point is that it should not be camouflaged as "the critical freedom of the gospel" but analytically and ideologically presented and justified in human political terms in the same way as our own option for socialism and a Marxist analysis.

We must bring together and summarize several points and arguments developed in this chapter concerning the relation of God's Kingdom and our concrete engagement in a particular historical project and course of action. This summary is, to be sure, only a tentative one, offered for further dialogue, but at the same time it is offered as theses related to our own Christian existence in Latin America today.

1. The positive relation between God's Kingdom and man's historical undertaking justifies us in understanding the former as a call to engage ourselves actively in the latter. The gospel invites and drives us to make concrete historical options and assures them eschatological permanence insofar as they represent the quality of human existence which corresponds to the Kingdom. We can, therefore, within human history, engage with other men in action which is significant in terms of God's redemptive purpose, of his announced and promised future Kingdom.

2. God's judgment encompasses the totality of our human achievements. But this is not meant to deter us from participating in the human enterprise but to liberate us for it, because we know that within and through this enterprise he will rescue what is significant and destroy what is negative. There is, therefore, also a critical and polemical dimension in the Christian witness which consists in bringing to judgment the human situation and assuming its conflicts and contradictions in terms of the realization of God's announced purpose.

3. Such a polemical and engaged participation necessarily implies a judgment between historical alternatives. This judg-

ment rests both on an understanding of the direction of God's redemptive will and an analytical and projective judgment of the present historical conditions. As to the former, although it is not possible to derive from the Scriptures any set of laws or principles for society, it is indeed possible and necessary to underline a *continuum*, a direction and a purpose in God's historical action as portrayed and interpreted in the Scriptures, which is conveyed through such expressions and symbols as "justice," "peace," "redemption" in their concrete biblical "illustrations." At the same time, it is equally necessary to stress the fact that such insights cannot be operative except in terms of historical projects which must incorporate, and indeed always do incorporate, an analytical and ideological human, secular, verifiable dimension.

4. The relation between the direction which we discover in God's witness in Scripture and tradition, the ideological projection which mobilizes man and gives a coherent project for action, and the analysis which guides and defines action is neither one-directional nor static. Science develops when it sets for itself human goals. These, in turn, can only be envisaged as science discloses the nature of the historical and natural process. New human possibilities lead us to enlarge our understanding of the biblical witness—indeed, in evangelical terms, the Spirit discloses Jesus Christ to us as we engage in the concrete witness to his redeeming love. But also the love which belongs to God's Kingdom suggests further horizons for human life which act as magnetic poles or horizons of hope for kindling man's analytical and ideological imagination.

5. This action of faith in kindling imagination is what has been called "the utopian function" of Christian eschatology. The name is not correct to the extent that the Kingdom is not *utopian:* it has a place both in history and in God's eschatological time. Moreover, the mobilizing visions of the future are also not utopian in the sense that they define projectively (both negatively and positively) the possibility for which we work in

the present. But, with these cautions, it can be said that the Christian faith provides today both a stimulus and a challenge for revolutionary action when it encourages us to look and work for historical realizations in the direction of the Kingdom in terms of justice, solidarity, the real possibility for men to assume responsibility, access of all men to the creation which God has given to man, freedom to create a human community through work and love, space to worship and play.

6. An eschatological faith makes it possible for the Christian to invest his life historically in the building of a temporary and imperfect order with the certainty that neither he nor his effort is meaningless or lost. In this context, the bold confession of the resurrection of the dead and the life everlasting is not a self-centered clinging to one's own life or a compensation for the sufferings of life or a projection of unfulfilled dreams but the confident affirmation of the triumph of God's love and solidarity with man, the witness to the enduring quality of man's responsible stewardship of creation and of his participation in love, the final justification of all fight against evil and destruction.

NOTES

[1] The main documents here are Engels's articles "On the History of Early Christianity," published in the journal *Neue Zeit* I/1-2 (1894-1895), pp. 4-13, 36-43. In English, *Marx and Engels on Religion* (Moscow: Foreign Language Publishing House, 1957), pp. 313-343.

[2] Juan L. Segundo, *Masas y minorías* (Buenos Aires: Editorial La Aurora, 1973), p. 67. Italics ours.

[3] Ibid., p. 71

[4] I have developed this view somewhat more extensively in a paper on "The Kingdom of God and History," to be published in Spanish in the book edited by C. René Padilla, *El Reino de Dios* (El Paso, Texas: Junta Bautista de Publicaciones, 1974).

[5] Jürgen Moltmann, *Theology of Hope: On the Ground and Implications of a Christian Eschatology* (New York: Harper & Row, 1967), see particularly the "Introduction: Meditation on Hope"), pp. 15-36.

[6] Cf. the discussion in *Diskussion über die 'Theologie der Hoffnung' von Jürgen Moltmann,* ed. Wolff-Dieter Marsch (Münich: Chr. Kaiser

Verlag, 1967). See also the criticisms of Rubem Alves (*A Theology of Human Hope*, pp. 55-68) and G. Gutiérrez (*A Theology of Liberation*, pp. 216-218).

[7] *The Crucified God,* see above, Chapter Six, no. 15.

[8] The discussion which follows addresses itself particularly to Chapter VIII of the book just mentioned, "Ways to the Political Liberation of Man" to which the quotations given correspond.

[9] Ibid., p. 304.

[10] Ibid., p. 298.

[11] Ibid., p. 300.

[12] Ibid., p. 302, summarizing, and concurring with, E. Peterson's argument.

[13] Ibid., p. 299.

[14] Ibid., p. 305.

[15] Ibid., p. 303.

[16] Ibid., p. 314.

Chapter Eight

Church, People,
and the Avant-Garde

At almost every point in our discussion the ecclesiological question was claiming a specific consideration. A Christian hermeneutics is unthinkable as a purely individual undertaking. It necessarily presupposes a "hermeneutical community." The discussion of class struggle raises the problem of the unity of the Church, and the relation between history and eschatology demands reflection on the location of the community of faith and confession in regard to both. We have postponed the specific discussion of the issue of faithfulness to the priorities of the theology of liberation as it has arisen in Latin America. The Church is, on the one hand, a basic fact which underlies all possible action and reflection: the life of the Church is the presupposition for the very existence of a Christian consciousness. On the other hand, a specific discussion on the nature of this community of faith can only come legitimately out of the engagement of Christians in the struggle for liberation. To put it in traditional philosophical terms: in our experience as Christians—and particularly as engaged Christians—the Church comes ontologically at the beginning but epistemologically at the end.

But, within this order, the discussion cannot be avoided, because the Church is the concrete and ineradicable witness to the "split of consciousness" which is intrinsic to the situation of the Christian, to the fact that his memory, his identity, his hope have a twofold reference—a total human reference and a particular Christian one—which in faith he confesses as one but empirically he experiences as an irreductible duality and tension. Both his integrity and his effectiveness are always threatened by this duality. But it would seem that he can only overcome this predicament at the cost of either his humanity or his faith. And, paradoxically, if he decides for one against the other he loses both! In our last chapter we looked at Moltmann's attempt to overcome this split, and indicated what we consider its insufficiency. The question, though, will not rest.

The theology of liberation shows unclearness and hesitations at the point of ecclesiology. There may be, as we shall later see, particular reasons for this. But we must begin by recognizing that the ecclesiological question is a critical one for all contemporary theology. The problem begins with the crisis of classical ecclesiologies—concretely the ecclesiologies of the Reformation and the Counter-Reformation—articulated in response to the question of the "true" over against the "false" Church. It presupposes a Christendom-situation and tries to establish criteria to justify the authenticity of one ecclesiastical body over against the rest. In a predominantly static, intellectualistic, and juridically minded frame of reference, the criteria adopted were backward-looking (historical, institutional, or demonstrable continuity with the past). Even the more dynamic attempts of Luther to insist on proclamation *(the viva vox evangelii)* and of Calvin to demand obedience (discipline) were soon frozen into a static and controllable doctrinal orthodoxy and puritanical moralism. Two interrelated factors, the growing dissolution of Christendom and the increasing consciousness of the historical character of the revelation and the Church, played havoc with this static conception. Pastoral and theological considerations encouraged a re-conception of the Church. The Dutch "theology of the apostolate" and ecumenical missionary theology rediscovered the mission-centered character of the New Testament understanding of the Church. In the midst of the struggle for a confessing Church, Bonhoeffer pointed to praxis[1]—which

155

in his concrete situation he identified as the protection of the rights of the Jews—as a sort of ecclesiological meta-criterion for the true Church, the mark of the Church-for-others or the servant-Church which points to its conformity to Christ. A real inversion has taken place: the eschatological vocation of the Church, its call to witness to the coming Kingdom, takes precedence over a static identity with its origin. Or, to put it more accurately, the origin is no longer seen as a set of foundational doctrines, structures, or norms but as the launching of a historical task which is drawn and oriented by its final destination.

This process of theological upheaval is accompanied, reflected, and forwarded by an ecclesial fluidity which makes traditional confessional criteria and institutional crystallizations largely irrelevant. The most significant fact in contemporary Christianity is the increasing "condensation" of the Christian consciousness around foci which express a certain way of understanding the character and demands of the gospel and of Christian life. One can speak of a "charismatic," of a "revolutionary," or a "conservation-oriented" understanding of Christian faith which cuts across all existing churches and denominations. Sometimes this happens within the structures of the churches, in other cases as para- or extra-ecclesiastical groups. In spite of the relative autonomy and localness of these various manifestations, it is possible to speak of "families" of Christian understanding and commitment which are slowly regrouping the Christian community. Whether this will mean the dissolution of the traditional institutional structures, their transformation, or a reconstitution of new ones, it is neither possible nor necessary to guess. But it seems justified to claim that we are living—in different sociological and cultural conditions—the kind of ecclesial fluidity and re-formation which characterized the sixteenth century. The impossibility to formulate a complete and neat ecclesiology is therefore neither accidental nor apt to be solved by a purely academic or intellectual effort. An untidy ecclesiological situation is the necessary expression of an untidy ecclesial situation and we should not strive to over-come it artificially.[2]

The best evidence of the depth of the crisis is the rapid theological and practical erosion of the most monolithic and best articulated of all classical ecclesiologies: that of the Roman Catholic Church. Less than a century after Vatican I had achieved the completion of the late medieval and Counter-Reformation understanding of the Church by firmly securing the keystone of the whole building, namely, papal primacy and infallibility, the countercurrents that finally surfaced at Vatican II succeeded in putting adrift the whole edifice by prefacing the juridical and institutional definitions of the Church with a mystical and communal understanding which did not take long, firstly, in relativizing and then radically challenging the older conception. It is in the context of this total situation that we must place the Latin American quest for a new ecclesiological understanding and a new ecclesial praxis.

To say that the Latin American theologians do not give high priority to the theological discussion of the Church does not mean that nothing has been said in this regard. We have already pointed to some significant insights in the theology of Gutiérrez, Gera, and Segundo. I shall now try to focus on the central aspects of these reflections and to sketch a criticism and advance some preliminary theses.

Gustavo Gutiérrez has lucidly described his own experience recounting how, from the common Christian and Catholic injunction to help the poor, he was led to understand Christian commitment as solidarity with the struggle of the poor for their liberation.[3] In Argentina, the Priests for the Third World have justified their option for Peronism by indicating that, as priests, they were called to serve the people, which means concretely to be solidary with the cause of the people—particularly the poor and dispossessed.[4] Instances could be multiplied: common to the new Christian awareness in the continent is the discovery of "the people," "the poor," "the oppressed," the vast masses of

157

marginal population as a fundamental call to the Christian. This experience is not only a sociological discovery. It takes on theological dimensions when seen in the light of Christ's special and foremost concern for the poor. The people become "a theological *locus*," the meeting place where Christ himself has promised to be present, the privileged sanctuary and sacrament of his presence. If the Church is where Christ is, do not the poor become constitutive of the mystery of the Church?

But we have repeatedly indicated that in Latin America we have understood the need to grasp theologically relevant historical facts by means of an adequate socio-analytical instrument. This means, concretely, that we can only see and serve the poor by understanding their situation as a class and participating in the struggle through which their alienation and oppression as a class can be overcome. In such a struggle we discover groups of people who have also undertaken—out of a certain ideology and a similar analysis—a leading participation in the quest for a new society. The Christian finds himself as a member of a community of historical commitment which not only cuts across denominational but also religious boundaries. He deeply experiences the reality of love, fellowship, sacrificial commitment, solidarity, and hope within this community in which the name of Jesus Christ is not invoked. If, nevertheless, this struggle must be assumed as a Christian service, as solidarity with Christ's own people—the poor—does not this revolutionary fellowship assume a certain "missionary," ecclesial character?

Furthermore, Christians engaged in a praxis of liberation are immediately thrown up against the ambiguous nature of their community of religious faith. We have already seen that prophetic denunciation on the part of the institutional Church of the conditions of oppression—such as that of Medellín, for instance—usually fails at the critical point of assuming the concrete struggle of the people. It has also become clear that this failure is closely related to the class alignment of both hierarchical structures and influential (in terms of power and money) lay groups in the churches. Finally, it is not difficult to detect the ideological use of the Christian influence as a weapon and protection in the effort to preserve the status quo. Their Christian commitment to the struggle of the poor therefore leads these Christians to the creation of an internal front within the community of faith. On the one hand, it is necessary to unmask the fact of class struggle as it takes place *within* the Church and, insofar as the sociologically mensurable entity that the Church is becomes or remains a part of the system of oppression, to "combat the Church" and work for its overthrow. On the other hand, the struggle for the poor discovers within the ecclesiatical institution—its organization, liturgy, forms of teaching—the factors of alienation and oppression that operate as a part of the religious life itself: the forms in which authority is exercised, the keeping of people in a state of permanent dependence and minority, the adoption of the competitive and individualistic criteria of the capitalist society. A Christian committed to liberation becomes therefore involved in the struggle for the reformation of the Church, or to put it more drastically, for the reconstitution of a Christianity in which all forms of organization and expression will be humanized and liberating.[5]

How can all these facts be integrated in a correct under standing of the Church and, even more important, in a correct ecclesial praxis? The attempts to find a point of entry for ecclesiological reflection have centered around the relation between "the Church of the oppressed," "the committed minority," and "the confessing community." Here, as in other realms, the theology of liberation strives to overcome all dualisms and to find the point of identity in these different circles of human community. One of the best expressions of this effort is the book of the French Dominican Benoit Dumas, who worked several years and wrote his book in Uruguay: *The Two Alienated Faces of the One Church.*[6] The main thesis is that "the poor"—understood in the total sociopolitical meaning of the concept, and applying a rigorous sociopolitical analysis—are not merely objects of Christian concern or an external entity to which the Church relates in one way or another, but an integral and structuring part of the mystery of the Church, as much as faith in Jesus Christ. Christ is present in the believer through faith and in the poor according to his promise. The whole doctrine of the Church must be thought out "between these two poles which question each other." The depth of the Church's alienation is plumbed by the fact that these two faces of the Church are separated from each other and in mutual opposition—the community of faith has become predominantly the Church of the rich and powerful and consequently the poor have been alienated from an explicit recognition of the Christ. The struggle for the *one* Church is the effort to bring together the two faces by keeping the christological center of the Church but at the same time rethinking the marks of the *ecclesia*—unity, visibility, catholicity—in terms of the presence of the suffering Christ in the poor. In his own simple and penetrating words:

> . . . the Church is not entirely within the Church—as long as the poor who await their liberation do not know the name of Jesus Christ and do not recognize him in his visible Body committed together with them; as long as those who hope in Christ and know his name do not know how to meet him, to name him, and to wait for him in the liberation of the poor.[7]

There are several ways of articulating theologically this basic ecclesiological insight. The form most frequently found among Latin American theologians is the one offered by the Vatican II when it speaks of the Church as the sacrament of mankind, or more accurately as "the sacrament of the salvation of mankind." This expression is meant to relate two theological insights. On the one hand, the Church is the visible manifestation of the history of salvation, the anticipatory presence of that which God intends to consummate for the whole of mankind. In this sense, the Church is the means through which God's saving will is manifested and achieved in history; it is the community of human destiny, to which all men belong by right and for which all are destined. On the other hand, it is the witness of God's saving action in the world, the place in which this universal activity of God—which takes place in all realms of human existence and activity—is manifested and interpreted. In this sense, the Church holds the meaning of human history.

While taking advantage of this notion, Latin American theologians are forced to revise it drastically. Two facts compel this modification. One is theological: the identification of God's saving action in the world in the struggle for liberation. The second is a fact of experience: the struggle for liberation is pioneered and carried forward by social classes and revolutionary movements among which Christians are a minority, while the churches are largely indifferent if not hostile to them. Among the theologians we have mentioned, several possibilities emerge. Segundo tends to remain closer to the Vatican II formulation: the whole of humanity is a "latent" Church moving toward a human fullness which coincides with the Christian gospel. But at the same time he radicalizes the meaning of the visible or confessing Church: it is the community (necessarily a minority) who grasps in faith the meaning of this human adventure and commits itself to the kind of existence and action that corresponds to it. The middle term "Christendom" or "nominal Christianity" is erased. We are left with the wider human community as the realm and scope of God's saving activity and the small Christian community of those committed to the costly service of love.[8] For Assmann, on the other hand, the decisive mark of the true Church is "the conscious emergence and the more explicit enacting of the one meaning of the one history,"[9] in other words, a revolutionary consciousness and commitment. The explicit reference to Jesus Christ becomes in this view gratuitous in the original sense of the word—something which is not demanded by or needed for the struggle—except in a sociological sense as the "Christian fact," freely and joyfully introduced by faith, plays a role in a given situation. The reference to Jesus Christ does not add an "extra" to the historical struggle but is totally and without rest identified with it.

To a certain extent one would have to say that the relation of Church and humanity portrayed by the Vatican II Council is in a way reversed: the secular struggle for the liberation of the poor discloses the meaning of the Church. This struggle becomes in one sense the true sacrament of God's historical saving activity, thus recalling the confessing community to its true meaning and destiny. We have seen how Benoit articulates this insight explicitly: only in the struggle for the liberation of the poor will the Church become the one true Church of Jesus Christ. In different ways, the theology of liberation seems to be saying this same thing. While I share this conviction, I find that the theological framework in which it is articulated is open to serious dangers.

On an elementary and practical level, this articulation fails to provide a theological location of and an adequate course of action in relation to the concrete and massive fact of the existing churches, the empirical organized institutions and communities in which the Christian heritage has been transmitted and is at present—at least formally—explicitly upheld and confessed. Some may tend to honor them verbally for strategic or tactical reasons, others to ignore them as irrelevant, still others to participate in them lukewarmly out of inertia, and some to denounce them as apostate. We shall see that there is a certain justification for some of these attitudes. But it seems to me that a Christian theology cannot prove itself adequate if it fails to grapple with the concrete facts of the ecclesiastical situation.

The inability we have just pointed out may possibly be traced back to a deeper problem: the imprecise and diffused identity given to the Church. Against the background of an exacerbated self-consciousness and a dominant or paternalistic attitude on the part of the churches, this shyness in making claims for the Church can be easily understood and supported. But is the answer to these distortions to be found in a blurring of that which distinguishes the Church *qua* Church of Jesus Christ from any other human group? Can we rest satisfied with a definition of the Church which coincides entirely with certain—real and important—needs formulated from an extra-ecclesiastical viewpoint? What is the meaning for the world of such a Church (except in a purely pragmatic, tactical game)? Is it possible to give to the face of the Church a greater definition without falling back on the imperialistic reflexes which the churches have so profoundly developed?

A clearer definition of the identity of the Church seems to me necessary not only—and perhaps not mainly—to safeguard the Church but for the sake of a genuine autonomy of the human struggle for liberation. When the cause of Jesus Christ (and consequently the Church in any missionary understanding of it) is totally and without rest equated with the cause of social and political revolution, either the Church and Jesus Christ are made redundant or the political and social revolution is clothed in a sacred or semi-sacred gown. Nonbelieving revolutionaries are then baptized as "latent," "crypto," "potential," or "unknowing" Christians, a new form of Christian paternalism which elicits a quite justified rejection on their part. On the other hand, given the fact that the sociopolitical revolution takes many and in some cases mutually divergent forms, how is the true Church to be identified? We seem to add the religious character of a "confessing war" to the differences arising from varying analytical, strategic, and tactical positions. This is no mere speculation. It becomes, in fact, increasingly difficult to communicate among groups of Christians who share the same socialist and revolutionary concern but who have chosen different paths for its realization.

It seems to me, therefore, that we must explore another theological framework for an understanding of the Church in a theology of liberation. In order to do so we must tie in our discussion of the unity and twofoldness of the total human history and the particular biblico-ecclesiastical history. The perfect singleness of history is a creational and an eschatological fact. We can at this point be helped by a vision such as that of Irenaeus of a single humanity created by God in order that it might grow toward full maturity. The goal of Christ's work is the relaunching of that movement in terms of the same orginal purpose. The problem then becomes how to understand the Church, holding fast both to the original, all-encompassing, and final unity of human history and to the particular density of the events gathered around the name of Jesus Christ.

In terms of such a purpose, we must ask ourselves whether in the articulations offered so far we have not remained prisoners of a contradiction. On the one hand, we have rightly emphasized the servant-character of the Church. On the other, we have attempted somehow to claim for the Church, or as Church, those who are "on the right" in terms of the movement of history. Have we not been in this respect still depending on the traditional dogma of *"extra ecclesia nulla salus"*? Have we not yielded to the old claim that the Church is destined to become the saved and definitive humanity? Perhaps we have expressed it in an apparently reversed (though also ancient) form, namely, that mankind is destined to become a universal Church. But the difference is finally not so great, because we draw in either case the consequence that all legitimate, authentically humanizing action bears the imprint of its ecclesial destiny and is therefore implicitly or explicitly, latently, if not visibly, Christian and churchly. We have renounced the attempt to subject all things to the ecclesiastical structure, but perhaps at the cost of sacralizing all human activity.

Is there an alternative theological framework? I think the question is not a purely theoretical one but a service demanded for the health of both the sociopolitical project and the faith of the Christians committed to it. We must be on our guard, at the same time, in order to avoid creating a purely artificial theological construction. The theological methodology we have defended requires that we develop theological theories in close relationship with the questions which arise out of the concrete historical praxis, and then look to the biblical and theological tradition in order that it may clarify such questions. The basic question posed for Christians politically committed is, in this respect, a certain tension, to which we have already alluded, in their relationships to a community of political engagement and to the community of Christian confession. In a very tentative and exploratory way I want to suggest a theological perspective which may help us to find our bearings in such a situation.

I think we must approach the theological tradition in terms of the relationship between the creational and the soteriological. Under the salutary influence of Karl Barth, most Protestant theology has practically buried this question under the epitaph of "natural theology." Barth's timely and needed defense of the freedom of the word does not, nevertheless, solve the problem, and he had himself to resort to notions like that of an *analogia fides,* and even *analogia relationis* to deal with the problems posed by ethics. We might ask whether we can't find a sound point of departure in the exploration of the relation between what some Reformed theologians called "the covenant of creation" and the "covenant of redemption."[10] Freely interpreted this would mean that mankind has been placed in a realm of responsibility which embraces a threefold free relationship to fellow men, to nature (the world), and to Yahweh (the God of the covenant). The Christian dispensation will then be understood in relation to such a covenant, as God's active will to restore man's relationships and responsibility, to reinstate him in his position as partner in the covenant of creation, to put him back again on the road of his self-realization.

The advantage of this approach is that it underlines the

significance of the soteriological without swallowing up the creational. Christ is not seen as a mere step in man's progress as in some evolutionist visions or as a semi-Gnostic mystical principle as in some cosmic christologies. On the other hand, this approach must be carefully set within the dynamic perspective which recent biblical, particularly Old Testament, research has lifted up. If creation—and human reality within it— is seen as a static, ready-made thing, the Christian dispensation might appear as a purely restorational device (the two-story view) or as an independent supra-historical realm (the two-kingdom idea). But if we take seriously the dynamic dimension inherent in the covenant-prophetic theology, the picture is altogether different. Creation is the installation of a movement; it is an invitation and a command to man to create his own history and culture, creatively to transform the world and make it into his own house and to explore the configurations of human relationships available to him.

When the realm of creation is understood in the terms we have sketched, the soteriological notions of sin and redemption gain a new meaning. They are seen in their truly accidental but crucial importance. Jesus Christ does not come to superimpose a different, transcendent, or celestial reality on top of the realm of nature and history, but to reopen for man the will and the power to fulfill his historical vocation. He has not come to make man into a superhuman being, or a religious creature, but to open to him the will and the power to be man. There is, to be sure, a certain provisionality and temporariness of the Christian dispensation implicit in this view. The German theologian Dorothee Soelle has offered in this respect a very valuable insight in her distinction between Christ as substitute—somebody who totally and permanently takes the place of another in relation to some task or function—and as representative—a person who temporarily and within limitations takes the representation of another *until* he is able to take his own representation and *in order that* he may do so.[11] Jesus' freedom before

166

God, his love for men, his power over nature are not an end in themselves, nor a merely substitutionary activity on our behalf but a truly representational function, in order that and until we ourselves may assume such relationships. Although we cannot here enter into a discussion of such christological interpretation, its New Testament ring will be easily perceived.

Faith in Christ is not, therefore, a step beyond humanity but toward it. "We are not men in order to be Christians, but Christians in order to be men."[12] In this soteriological order, the Church has a distinct but provisional and subordinate place. It is commissioned to proclaim God's salvation in Jesus Christ. This means, in traditional terms, the forgiveness of sins, namely, man's freedom in God's grace to take up again, in whatever circumstances and after whatever failure and destruction, the work committed to him in creation. It means, also in traditional terms, the call to the sanctification of man, namely, the invitation to effective love and the freedom to love. The Church is itself when it witnesses to God's saving activity in Jesus Christ, that is, when it makes clear God's renewed authorization, commandment, and liberation to man to be human, to create his own history and culture, to love and to transform the world, to claim and exercise the glorious freedom of the children of God. The Church's distinct—and certainly scandalous—claim is that the fullness of this humanity is given in the explicit, faithful, and grateful acknowledgment of Jesus Christ.

Lest everything we have just said be misunderstood, two things must be made clear. The first is that proclamation and faith always take place in history and as historically defined actions. In traditional philosophical language, we would say that there is no purely formal announcement of God's graceful invitation to man. It is always a concrete project for human existence, embodied—whether the Church is conscious of it or not—in a particular political, ideological option. It is, at the same time, an invitation to dare to be, in God's freedom, a lord or a servant, a bourgeois or a revolutionary, a man of yesterday or a man of tomorrow. And this is not merely done verbally but given in the total insertion of a Church in history, in its total praxis, in the way in which it is located and it locates itself in the power-field of contemporary historical conflicts. The question of proclamation is, therefore, always the question as to the praxis of faith of the Church, as to the historical option in which this faith is embodied. Transcendence, as we have already discussed, can only be found from within such a praxis, never as a super-added, disembodied x. The historical imprint of faith in a given human praxis—which may and should become visible—can only be recognized *by others* and *when it takes place.* It cannot be prescribed beforehand! This is—if I understand him correctly—what Bonhoeffer meant by "living before God as if God did not exist."

The second point to clarify has to do with the often debated question of the "men of good will" or the non-Christians who embrace the same liberating historical praxis. Curiously enough we have reversed the biblical concern with this problem. The service of love, the trust and goodness of the nonbeliever, is presented in the Bible not as a problem but as a sign of God's free and universal grace and as a call to repentance and conversion. Humility and praise, not confusion, is the proper response to the experience of the selflessness, generosity, and faithfulness of the nonbeliever who militates at our side. As an aside, one should add that this does not apply only to individuals and groups but to the total historical process. Why should we be concerned and bewildered when man takes into his own hands the humanization of life—physical and mental health, the regularization of nature, the future of the human race? Our only concern is for the full responsibility of man, not the vindication of some restricted sphere for God (and for ourselves as his representatives). Insofar as he really believes, the Christian is not afraid of becoming superfluous, as Jesus was not when he promised to his disciples: "He who believes in me will do the works I do, nay, he will do greater works than mine, because I go to the Father" (John 14:12).

The Church, that is, the fellowship of those who embrace a historical task in the freedom of God's forgiveness and sanctification, cannot exist except as it concretely celebrates this freedom, reflects on it, and proclaims it. This is the meaning of the *disciplina arcana,* the specific and peculiar practices of the confessing community which the same Bonhoeffer who invited us to live "without religion" valued so highly. Such discipline has no meaning except insofar as it is related to, indeed as it is constituted by, the concrete creational praxis of these Christians. But such praxis has no Christian meaning—which does not mean that it does not have historical significance—unless it is celebrated in the community of faith. Eschatologically, to be sure, the distinction disappears, because this distinction measures what still is missing in our full humanity. There is no distinct worship, reflection, or proclamation at the end. There is no temple in the New Jerusalem. Nobody needs to say to his brother "Know the Lord" (Jer. 31:34). But we live before the *millennium.* In Marxist terms we would say: we live in the pre-history of mankind. Just as in history there will not be separate art and artists, no separate literature, no need for a reflection of human life in order to grasp it, so when the true human time comes there will be no need for a reflection of God. The time of the Messiah will have ended and "we shall know even as we are known." Between the times, though, still in pre-history, the Church must project its historical praxis in a distinct celebration, reflection, and proclamation in order to renew for itself and for the world the knowledge of God's authorization and invitation to be human.

If the ecclesiological lines we have sketched are anywhere near the truth, certain pastoral or practical ecclesiological consequences seem to follow, which deserve to be mentioned. These points are only offered as questions raised for the future of the Christian community in our situation.

If there is no faith except as embodied in a concrete historical praxis, we must see ecclesiology *as a conflict for the true Church,* as the confrontation of concrete historical options embraced as the obedience that faith is. At the same time we recognize that as Christians we are engaged in different and contradictory options. The existing ecclesiastical institutions and communities will not be seen, therefore, as complete and stable entities, but as the field in which the struggle for the Church takes place. To belong faithfully to the Church means to claim our place within this field and to engage in the struggle for a true, faithful, historical obedience. It is in this context that the question of unity is posed. The question of the true unity of the Church is authentic only when it is at the same time the question of the true separation, when it gathers and separates Christians in the conflict of confession—a confession which is a concrete historical praxis. The true quest for unity is not therefore to be found in the negotiations of ecclesiastical bodies—which are only a field, not the real contenders—but in this conflict and encounter which takes place within and across them.

A concrete ecclesiology cannot ignore the practical significance of the tension introduced by what we have called the pre-eschatological or pre-historic nature of Christian and churchly existence. Christians experience life as a tension between the proper weight of their concrete historical option, which tends to become self-contained and absolute and the Christ-reference in that praxis which always threatens to become religious (i.e., a substitute). The attempt to eliminate this tension cannot but be fatal. Once the tension is admitted, though, it is necessary to attempt to make it fruitful. It seems that one way of doing it is to recognize that Christians live their identity as such in different levels which go from their personal historical commitment to their corporate confession of Christ. I find that in this respect the old distinction between "the Christian" and "the Church" has a certain limited validity and usefulness.

At the corporate level—namely, in the communal and organized existence as Church—the dominant dimension is the *explicit* reference to Jesus Christ; it is the realm of confession, worship, proclamation. But it cannot be forgotten that it is the explicit reference to Jesus Christ of a concrete historical praxis. The Church cannot therefore, precisely in its corporate existence, forgo a definite option. There is no worship, no confession, no proclamation above right and left, beyond oppression and liberation, in a classless heaven. A Church becomes a community of faith in decision. And this decision places it for or against Christ. This apparently fanatical assertion needs to be clarified in at least three directions: (1) by placing it in historical perspective and realizing that this has in fact taken place always, and particularly, at the times when the Christian faith has been alive and significant in human history; (2) by rejecting all fanaticism and recognizing that a Christian option cannot take place except through mediations—a theological and ethical reflection which incorporates a certain analytical and ideological understanding of history into a careful and intelligent listening to the word of Scripture and the tradition of the Church; and (3) by requiring a certain latitude in the definition of a corporate Christian option; in this respect we can speak of certain "families of options," such as is suggested by the differences in the tactical and even strategic positions of the Christian groups we have identified in the earlier part of the book.

At the personal level—i.e., as Christians placed within particular contexts—the dominant dimension is the "creational" one, the specific strategic and tactical option, and usually the Christ-reference is mostly *implicit*. A Christian does not cease to be such at this level of life, nor does he cease to be a witness of Jesus Christ or a "presence" of the Church—the Church in *diaspora* as it has been frequently said. His faith, hope, and love should find concrete reflection in his praxis. But this reflection will be (generally) totally incorporated in this praxis. Only faith discerns the presence of Jesus Christ!

Between the two extremes, the corporate-institutional level and the personal, there is place for a number of ecclesial configurations: small communal groups of Christians sharing a particular political commitment (a party or a tactical option), groups of Christians and non-Christians interested in exploring the relation of their commitment to the Christian faith, occasional massive gatherings of Christians to witness to their Christian conviction in relation to some particular contemporary event (i.e., the meetings of Christian solidarity with the people of Chile after the fascist coup, which took place in several countries, or the meetings of "Christians for socialism" in Chile or in Spain). The constitution of such groups, frequently called "para-ecclesiastical" or "extra-ecclesiastical" or even "underground" or "irregular," has been quite widespread during the last few years. We cannot now enter a discussion of them. It is quite important not to lump them all together. There is a wide difference between introverted groups which still move basically in the subjective and intersubjective sphere of bourgeois religiosity (however "protesting" or uncommon their expression may look) and groups which have moved into a political space and relate their communal Christian experience to a concrete political and ideological praxis.

The importance of these manifestations ought to raise a substantial theological point, which words like "para-" or "extra-" ecclesiastical tend to conceal. If the Church is in fact that which happens in the struggle for the true faith-obedience which takes place within the "field" of the formal explicit confession of Jesus Christ, should we not recognize that "Church" is an analogical term covering a number of different instances? In a way we have always admitted it by using the same word for a local congregation, a denomination, the "universal Church," or national churches. But a static ecclesiology has always tried to erect one of these instances into a normative one and establish a sort of "relative ecclesial density" in relation to it. Such an assumption is immediately relativized in a sociological and historical perspective. What we really have are historical and time-bound "condensations" of the struggle to confess Jesus Christ significantly throughout history. These varied ecclesial formations that we have just enumerated belong within this struggle and therefore are in their own right "churchly" as much as any national, denominational, or local Church. In fact, it is only as Christians seek together—in a common historical commitment celebrated in praise and confession—the obedience that faith is, does the face of Jesus Christ acquire identifiable features in a given time. This is what has happened in history and this is what is happening now, for instance, in Latin America and Africa, or among the black in the U.S.A.

The question of a Christology of liberation or a spirituality of liberation, real and urgent as it is, is dependent on the existence of such movements, groups, and manifestations as those we have indicated. It cannot be artificially constructed in a theological laboratory or in a devotional hothouse. As Martin Luther King went out to the streets singing "We shall overcome" or as Puerto Rican Christians represented the *via crucis* on Good Friday, the spirituality or the Christology of liberation emerges. Theological reflection will articulate it, make explicit its reference to the sources, and ask the critical questions necessary for its correction. But the matrix will only be found where Christians celebrate and confess together their quite earthly, immediate, and concrete commitment to the liberation of man. There is no other way of knowing Jesus Christ. He himself forewarned us: "He who wills to do [God's] will shall know my doctrine . . . " (John 7:17).[13]

NOTES

[1] This point about Bonhoeffer's ecclesiology is emphasized in André Dumas, *Une théologie de la réalité* (Geneva; Labor et Fides, 1968).
[2] For some remarks concerning the ecclesiological and ecumenical question in Latin America, cf. my article, "A Latin American attempt

to locate the question of unity" (Geneva, Faith and Order Documents, FO/73:37, October, 1973).

[3] *Fe y cambio social en América Latina,* pp. 230 ff.

[4] Cf. *Polémica en la Iglesia* (Buenos Aires: Búsqueda, 1970).

[5] Cf. Alegría, *Yo creo en la esperanza,* pp. 141 ff.

[6] *Los dos rostros alienados de la Iglesia una* (Buenos Aires: Latino-américa Libros, 1971).

[7] Ibid., p. 20.

[8] Cf. *supra,* pp. 62-65.

[9] *Opresión-Liberación,* p. 22

[10] For this formulation I am particularly indebted to my colleague Lambert Schuurman.

[11] *Christ the Representative* (London: S.P.C.K., 1969).

[12] The expression is often quoted by Lambert Schuurman.

[13] We should still reflect on Albert Schweitzer's conclusion of his epoch-making study of the research for the historical Jesus: ". . . to those who obey Him, whether they be wise or simple, He will reveal Himself in the toils, the conflicts, the sufferings which they shall pass through in His fellowship, and, as ineffable mystery, they shall learn in their own experience Who He is." *The Quest of the Historical Jesus* (London: T. & T. Black, 1926), p. 401.

Bibliography

What follows is a selection indicative of specifically theological Latin American works of the last ten years, directly related to the development of a theology of liberation. Only those items have been included which are more readily available. No historical or sociological references are included. The notes in the text will help the interested reader to discover further relevant material.

BIBLIOGRAPHIES:

Alvarez Bolado, J. "Bibliografía de la teología de la liberación." In *Fe Cristiana y Cambio Social en America Latina.* Salamanca: Editorial Sígueme, 1973, pp. 410 ff.

"Bibliografía de la Teología de la Liberación." In *Boletín Bibliográfico Iberoamericano.* Madrid, OCHSA, 1972.

CIDOC. *Document I/1, 73/386.* Centre for Intercultural Documentation, Apartado 479, Cuernavaca, México.

Facelina, R. "Liberation and Salvation; International Bibliography." *RIC Supplement,* no. 3, CERDIC Publications, 9 Pl. de l'Université, 67084, Strasbourg, France; 1973, 35 pp.

Vanderhoff, F.-P. *Bibliography: Latin American Theology of Liberation.* Ottawa, mimeo., 1973.

COMPOSITE WORKS, SYMPOSIA, SPECIAL ISSUES OF JOURNALS:

Aportes para la Liberación. Bogotá: Presencia, 1970, 144 pp.; *Opción de la Iglesia latino-americana en la década del 70.*

Bogotá: Presencia, 1970, 115 pp. The first volume reproduces the papers and the second the preparatory documents of the "Symposium on the theology of liberation" held in Bogotá, 6–7 March, 1970. Some of the authors are G. Gutiérrez, Mgr. Proaño, F. Hinkelammert, G. Pérez Ramírez.

C.E.L.A.M. *La Iglesia en la actual transformación de América a la luz del Concilio:* 1. *Ponencias;* 2. *Conclusiones.* Medellín: C.E.L.A.M. Publications, 2 vols., 1968. Preparatory materials and conclusions of the Second Latin American Conference of Bishops (Roman Catholic).

Cristianismo y Sociedad. Journal of ISAL., Church and Society in Latin America, published in Montevideo, Uruguay. Vol. VIII, nos. 24–25, 1970 and vol. IX, nos. 26–27, 1971 are devoted to the theology of liberation and include articles by J. de Santa Ana, G. Gutiérrez, H. Assmann, Rubem A. Alves, O. Fals Borda, K. Lenkensdorf, P. Blanquart.

Los cristianos y la revolución: un debate abierto en América Latina. Santiago: Editorial Quimantu, 1972, 393 pp.

Cristianos por el socialismo. Santiago, Chile: Editorial Mundo Nuevo, 1972, 302 pp. The official text of the preparatory documents, addresses and proceedings of the "Primer Encuentro de Cristianos por el Socialismo."

Cristianos por el socialismo: Exigencias de una opción. Montevideo: Editorial Tierra Nueva, 1973, 165 ˙pp. Evaluation and discussion of the "Primer Encuentro de Cristianos por el Socialismo"; articles by H. Assmann, L. Bach, J. Blanes, J. Míguez Bonino, J. Girardi, et al.

Explosives Lateinamerika. Edited by Theo Tschuy. Berlin: Kreuz Verlag, 1969. A collection of articles, mostly by Protestant authors, including J. Barreiro, E. Castro, J. de Santa Ana, J. Míguez Bonino, L. Odell.

Fe Cristiana y Cambio Social en América Latina. Edited by J. Alvarez Bolado. Salamanca: Editorial Sígueme, 1973, 428 pp. Text of addresses and proceedings of the seminars of the "Encuentro de El Escorial" (Spain, July, 1972). One of the most important gatherings of people related to theological work; L.A. papers by H. Assmann, L. Borrat, J. Comblin, E. Dussel, S. Galilea, G. Gutiérrez, J. Scannone, A. Buntig, J. Míguez Bonino et al.

Gheerbrandt, Alain. *La Iglesia rebelde de América Latina.* Mexico: Editorial Siglo XXI, 1970, 319 pp. A collection of statements, letters, and pronouncements by Roman Catholic individuals and groups in Latin America in relation to the Medellín Conference of bishops, and reflecting the social concern. Originally published in French: *L'É-glise rebelle de l'Amérique Latine.* Paris: Editions du Seuil, 1969.

Pueblo Oprimido, Señor de la Historia. Edited by H. Assmann. Montevideo: Editorial Tierra Nueva, 1972, 270 pp. Preparatory papers and presentations at the ISAL symposium in Buenos Aires, June, 1971. Papers by H. Assmann, P. Blanquart, K. Lenkersdorf, O. Fals Borda, N. Olaya, J. de Santa Ana, J. Míguez-Bonino, L. Rivera Pagan, J. Croatto, et al.

Rossi, J. J. and Segundo, J. L. *Iglesia Latinoamericana, ¿protesta o profecía?* Buenos Aires: Búsqueda, 1969, 462 pp. A dossier of documents from seventeen Latin American countries between 1968-69 by bishops, episcopal conferences, groups of priests and laymen "contesting" social conditions and structural problems in Church and in society. An introduction by J. L. Segundo.

Stromata (Journal of the Faculty of Theology of the Jesuit "Universidad de El Salvador"; Buenos Aires, Argentina). "Liberación Latinoamericana," 1972, nos. 1-2, pp. 1-193.

Papers presented in a symposium by H. Assmann, H. Borrat, E. Dussel, and J. Scannone.

INDIVIDUAL WORKS:

Alves, Rubem. *A Theology of Human Hope.* Washington, D.C.: Corpus Books, 1969. Also published in Portuguese and in Spanish.

———. *Tomorrow's Child.* New York: Harper & Row., 1972.

Araya, Victor. *Fe cristiana y marxismo.* Mimeographed; San José, Costa Rica: Universidad de Costa Rica, 1973. A thesis submitted to the University of San José, Costa Rica.

Assmann, Hugo. *Opresión-Liberación: Desafío a los cristianos.* Montevideo: Editorial Tierra Nueva, 1972, 111 pp.

———. *Teología desde la praxis de liberación.* Salamanca: Editorial Sígueme, 1973, 271 pp. Includes the preceding item and adds several essays.

Barreiro, Julio. *Ideología y cambios sociales.* Montevideo: Editorial Tierra Nueva, 1966.

Cámara, Dom Helder. *Church and Colonialism.* London and Sidney: Sheed and Ward, 1969, 181 pp. Translation from Portuguese.

———. *Revolution through Peace.* New York: Harper & Row, 1972, 159 pp. Translation from Portuguese.

Dussel, Enrique. *América Latina: Dependencia y Liberación.* Buenos Aires: Fernando Garcia Cambeiro, 1973, 228 pp.

———. *Caminos de Liberación Latinoamericana.* Buenos Aires: Latinoamérica Libros, 1972, 174 pp.

———. *Historia de la Iglesia en América Latina.* Barcelona: Editorial Nova Terra, 1972, 348 pp.

Eggers Lan, Conrado. *Cristianismo, Marxismo y Revolución Social.* Buenos Aires: Jorge Alvarez, 1964, 95 pp.

Gutiérrez, Gustavo. *Praxis de Liberación y Fe Cristiana.* Lima, Peru: Centro de Documentación MIEI-JECI, 1972, 28 pp.

————. *A Theology of Liberation.* Maryknoll, New York: Orbis Books, 1973, 323 pp. Original Spanish, *Teología de la Liberación.* Lima: Editorial Universitaria, 1971, 376 pp.

Miranda, José Porfirio, S. J. *Marx y la Biblia. Crítica a la filosofía de la opresión.* Mexico: Edición del autor, Rio Hondo 1, Mexico 20, D.F., 1971, 261 pp. Second edition by Sígueme, Salamanca, 1972, 342 pp.

————. *El Ser y el Mesías.* Salamanca: Sígueme, 1973.

Ossa, Leonor. *Die Revolution—das ist ein Buch und ein freier Mensch.* Hamburg: Furche Verlag, 1973, 173 pp.

Segundo, Juan Luís. *Acción Pastoral Latinoamericana: sus motivos ocultos.* Buenos Aires: Ediciones Búsqueda, 1972.

————. *Masas y minorías.* Buenos Aires: Editorial La Aurora, 1973.

————. *De la sociedad a la teología.* Buenos Aires: Ediciones Carlos Lohlé, 1970, 180 pp.

————. *Teología abierta para el laico adulto.* 5 vols. Buenos Aires, Ediciones Carlos Lohlé. The five volumes written in cooperation at the "Centro P. Fabbro" are:

Esa comunidad llamada Iglesia. 1968, 258 pp. E.T.: *The Community Called Church.* Maryknoll, New York: Orbis Books, 1972.

Gracia y condición humana. 1969, 308 pp. E.T.: *Grace and the Human Condition.* Maryknoll, New York: Orbis Books, 1973.

Nuestra Idea de Dios. 1970, 266 pp.

Los Sacramentos Hoy. 1971, 206 pp.

Evolución y Culpa. 1972, 258 pp.

(E.T. of the last three volumes forthcoming in Orbis Books.)

Torres, Camilo. *Revolutionary Priest: The Complete Writings & Messages of Camilo Torres.* Edited by John Gerassi. New York: Random House, Vintage, 1971.